PANOS

LET THE
DAWN COME

SOCIAL DEVELOPMENT:
LOOKING BEHIND THE CLICHÉS

© Panos London 1995

Published by Panos Publications Ltd
9 White Lion Street
London N1 9PD, UK

British Cataloguing in Publishing Data
A catalogue record for this book is available from the British Library

Extracts may be freely reproduced by the press or non-profit organisations, with or without acknowledgement. Panos would appreciate clippings of published material based on the book.

Let the Dawn Come — Social development: looking behind the clichés was commissioned and edited by Simon Burne, executive director of Panos, 1992-94, with final editing by Wendy Davies.

Funding for this book was provided by Novib. The views expressed by the authors do not necessarily reflect the views and policies of the funding agency.

Panos London is an independent information organisation working internationally for development that is socially, environmentally and economically sustainable. Panos also has offices in Paris and Washington DC.

For more information about Panos contact Juliet Heller.

Production: Sally O'Leary with Barbara Cheney
Managing editor: Heather Budge-Reid
Cover design: Sally O'Leary with John McGill
Cover photograph: T. Bølstad
Additional picture research: Adrian Evans and Teresa Woloiec
Printed in Great Britain by Bell and Bain, Glasgow

Contents

Preface

We are moving quickly through the fourth decade of development. Although the last 35 years have seen progress on many fronts, the scale of human misery does not diminish significantly. Indeed, in the last decade, development indices have been falling in many of the poorest countries.

Perhaps we have been trying to go too fast. We wanted an end to all that was wrong in the world faster than any development programme could deliver. Each decade has brought with it its own cure for the ills of underdevelopment but none has achieved what it hoped for.

With the end of the Cold War, there were high hopes of a peace dividend and the freeing of money to finance urgent human development programmes around the world. Instead, conflicts have proliferated and development assistance is declining in real terms.

The Social Summit in Copenhagen in March 1995 offers a chance to take a more positive development path. Fundamental to this is a re-allocation of resources. Less than a quarter of the current global expenditure on arms would be enough to finance a programme for universal primary health care, vaccination against killer diseases, drinking water and primary schooling.

The UN conference seeks to promote "social development", or "people-centred development", with programmes to tackle poverty, provide basic social services, allocate land and resources more fairly, and create employment. A central concern is social integration—so that all people, including underprivileged minorities, can participate in defining their own future and enjoy the fruits of development.

How best to meet these challenges will continue to be the subject of much debate. As the World Bank itself has said, "perhaps the clearest lesson from work on development during the past 30 years is that there is a premium on pragmatism and an open mind [1]." It needs to dawn on all of us that there is no one answer to development: that each culture, each community, each country must have the power, resources and confidence to mould their own paths of development.

Too often, assumptions are made about what the poor want, or their views are interpreted to such a point that they bear little relationship to the development priorities originally identified by the poor. We need to be humbler in our approach, though no less determined to overcome the iniquities that beset our world. This goes as much for the international community as for national governments, north and south, and as much for non-government organisations as for multilateral institutions.

This book has been written by journalists from the five countries featured. Trained to observe, listen and investigate, they spent time in communities, listening to what people had to say. Each was equipped only with a tape recorder, to ensure a faithful transcription of people's words, and was accompanied by a photographer, also from the same country.

All those interviewed have been part of specific development initiatives. Each of the organisations described here was created locally and is non-governmental. Each attempts, in different ways, to encourage the active participation of the people they seek to benefit. This means that the people interviewed already have experience of speaking out.

The contribution of this volume is to help ensure that the voices of ordinary people are not lost, and that they reach a wider audience. The book attempts to bridge the huge gulf that often exists between what development professionals think, say and do and what ordinary people want out of development. In the words of Elina Ncube in Zimbabwe, it is "a meeting of the brains." It brings together farmer and researcher, development worker and government official.

I believe that valuable lessons can be learnt from the experiences related, but only if they are applied and adapted in appropriate ways. Let us not use this volume to develop a new model of development, but rather as a companion to help us on our development journey.

Looking behind the clichés and listening to people's experiences in their complexity and diversity—may begin to lead to a new dawning of understanding.

Juan Somavia
Ambassador, Permanent Representative of Chile to the United Nations, Chairperson of the Preparatory Committee of the World Summit for Social Development.

Acknowledgements

Panos wishes to acknowledge the help given by many individuals and organisations across the world in compiling this collection. Thanks go to Novib for their support of the project, and particularly to Claudia Zeiske, Allert van der Ham, Caroline Wildeman and Max van den Berg. Thanks to Mick Howes, Stephen Biggs, Nicole Brown, Carmen Miranda, Aida Opuku-Mensah, Susan Bretherton, Kitty Warnock, Liz Carlile and James Dean for advice and comments. Thanks also to Daniel Nelson, Wafula Oguttu, Leonard Maveneka, Nancy McGirr, Laurence Jay Spear and Adrian Evans for advice on names of journalists and photographers. Finally, thanks for their patience and support to the heads and all the staff of IDESI, CDRO, FIDA, ORAP, JSK/PBKMS/SMS and Proshika.

Candles in the Wind

Forces for and against social development

In any field, it is important to draw up guidelines for "best practice", and development is no exception to this rule. There is no shortage of writers doing just this: analysing and commenting on the wide-ranging development efforts of the tens of thousands of organisations working to improve the lot of the world's poor. But very seldom do we hear directly from the poor themselves. Their views are usually interpreted and filtered through the fine sand of intellectual analysis to the point where often little remains of what was originally said.

This book seeks to redress the balance through a selection of studies which draw out the experiences, needs and aspirations of a small sample of ordinary women and men from five different developing countries. The testimonies point to some of the priorities and pitfalls facing development workers and give some indication of where we should be placing our efforts.

The majority of people whose voices are heard in this book have directly benefited from—or been affected by—the work of a non-government organisation (NGO). These organisations are: in Guatemala, the Association for Cooperation and the Rural Development of Western Guatemala (CDRO); in Uganda, the International Federation of Women Lawyers (FIDA); in Bangladesh, Proshika; in Zimbabwe, the Organisation of Rural Associations for Progress (ORAP); and in India, the Centre for People's Solidarity (JSK), the West Bengal Agricultural

Labourers' Association (PBKMS) and a parallel organisation for women labourers (SMS).

The NGOs are engaged in a wide range of activities, including community development, employment and income generation, and campaigning for legal rights. They are all very different, as are the communities they serve. Yet there are also important similarities, which this chapter will seek to explore.

The views in this book are very personal: they reflect the deep concerns and hopes of the people interviewed. With few exceptions, people do not talk directly about global issues such as debt or structural adjustment. They do, however, talk about the government policies that arise from these problems: the rising cost of school fees, the lack of government services, falling employment and the rising price of food.

The wider context

While this book seeks to draw out best practice for the implementation of social development programmes, it is clear that real development will take place only when there is a fundamental change in the global economic system. Good development programmes can create "pools of development", benefiting particular communities or groups of people, but they will be little more than candles lighting an otherwise dark cavern unless we address the wider forces that affect them.

And the candles can easily be snuffed out. The most apparently sustainable development programme can be destroyed by forces outside the control of the community. ORAP's programme in Zimbabwe has been derailed by drought, the scars of war are still clearly visible in Guatemala and Uganda, while Bangladesh is regularly beset by cyclones and flooding. One test of any development programme must be the extent to which communities can overcome these disasters and rebuild.

The Action Agenda and Social Charter (see Appendices 1 and 2), proposed by the United Nations Development Programme (UNDP) for discussion at the 1995 UN Social Summit, could help us to light more candles and protect them from the winds of destruction, but only if the rhetoric is followed by concerted action, and the prioritisation of programmes which specifically benefit the poor.

The arms trade from North to South is still worth three times more than official development assistance (ODA). Four per cent of the money spent on defence by developing countries could halve the adult illiteracy rate, provide universal primary education and educate women to the same level as men. Twelve per cent would provide primary health care for all (including immunisation of all children against major preventable diseases), eliminate severe malnutrition and halve moderate malnutrition, and provide safe drinking water for all [1].

The richest 20% of the world's population earns 61 times as much as the poorest 20% [2]. The gap between rich and poor worldwide has doubled over the last 30 years. Clearly, since the vast majority of poor people live in the South, it cannot be justified that from 1983 to 1992 an average of US$14.7 billion a year flowed from developing countries to the rich North [3].

Compounding this gross inequity is the fact that within developing countries too, there is an ever-widening chasm between rich and poor. The structural adjustment programmes (SAPs) introduced in the 1980s in many countries of the South have forced a dramatic slowdown in government-funded social programmes in health, education, infrastructure and employment. At the same time they have opened up the poorest economies to imports of manufactured goods from the North. Farmers are encouraged to grow cash crops for export to generate the foreign exchange required for the purchase of imports which they themselves cannot afford to buy.

Debt servicing and repayment remain a heavy burden on developing countries. Most have, however, achieved a small reduction in their foreign debt: as a percentage of Gross National Product (GNP), debt decreased on average from 23% in 1987 to 21% in 1991 [4]. However, in sub-Saharan Africa this proportion rose from 11% in 1980 to 26% in 1991. Thus the poorest nations are slipping further into debt, forcing even more emphasis on to cash crops and away from food production.

Not all the news is bad. Life expectancy in developing countries rose on average from 46.2 years in 1960 to 63 in 1992—

Liba Taylor/Panos Pictures

Structural adjustment programmes are forcing governments to cut spending on essential programmes such as health.

an increase of 36% in little over a generation—and even in sub-Saharan Africa it rose from 40 to 51.1 years. Smallpox has been eradicated. Infant mortality dropped from 149 per 1,000 live births to 69 over the same period—a halving of the rate. Literacy rates and school enrolments have all improved significantly [5].

Yet, in recent years, particularly in sub-Saharan Africa, there are fears that many of these hard-won gains are being jeopardised, if not lost. AIDS is affecting increasing numbers of people from the most economically productive age group and is increasing the strain on already stretched health budgets, while care of AIDS patients places an enormous pressure on families and on government services. SAPs are forcing large cutbacks in essential health and education programmes, and ODA is insufficient to fill the gaps. The UN target for ODA of 0.7% of GNP for all developed countries has been achieved by fewer than 10 countries, and many have reduced their ODA in real terms. Moreover, international NGOs are finding it increasingly difficult to raise the additional funds needed for their work.

As important as the quantity of ODA is its quality. Too much aid is wasted on grandiose schemes, or spent on political priorities rather than on alleviating poverty. On average, only 7% of the bilateral aid from Northern governments goes to fund programmes in basic primary education, primary health care, mass-coverage water supply systems and family planning services. If donors raised that percentage to 20%, as called for by UNDP, this would provide an additional US$8 billion a year for essential social programmes [6].

The first axiom of development support is that it should be flexible, able to meet the changing needs and priorities of communities. Evaluation of programmes is important but will work only if beneficiaries are involved in the process; expensive and time-consuming reviews undertaken by outside consultants are not the answer. Second, support needs to be long-term. Organisations should make their commitment clear from the outset, and need to assess the success of their assistance over a reasonable period of time, 5-10 years at least. Third, there needs to be a commitment to a way of working that is interactive. There are always outside ideas that can stimulate community action. But a real partnership occurs only when both parties feel free to accept or reject the advice or the involvement of the other.

This book gives examples of how aid can be put to good effect for the benefit of the poorest. While it is impossible to fix hard and fast criteria by which development programmes should be judged, it is evident that certain themes—such as employment, social services, food security, land rights, participatory working methods, scaling up and sustainability— arise repeatedly. These issues are examined in the rest of this chapter.

Participation

Participation is seen currently as the panacea for people's development. But it is clear that, for many, the term is becoming a useful label—like empowerment and many other development slogans before it—which enables things to go on much the same as before. For some, participation is seen simply as an effective means of getting a particular message across.

Participation is fundamentally about power: the power to make decisions affecting one's own life, and the life and development of the community; the power to say "no", as well as

Jeremy Hartley/Panos Pictures

Participation requires the establishment of new structures whose foundation is village-level groups.

to say "yes". It is not just a convenient mechanism to ensure that projects work better.

Two points concerning participation emerge in this book. First, service provision is effective only if there are participative structures which enable people to define their needs and priorities and the way in which they want those needs met: participation is therefore fundamental to the whole development process. Second, the services provided do not themselves need to be participatory: indeed, people are asking for services which they can use in the way that best suits their circumstances and priorities. The role of government as provider of these services is still seen as crucial. Apart from anything else, communities simply do not have the time or skills to undertake all these activities themselves.

Collective action usually fails if it is organised through existing power structures. The old elites may simply predominate: the rich over the poor, the powerful over the weak, men over women. People want to work with their close family members, the immediate community, other landless people, other women. The question of who benefits is a vital one, since participation on its own does not ensure that the poorest will get what they want.

Both NGOs and governments need to give much more support than they do currently to the structures that ensure participation, and then to concentrate on providing services defined by these structures. The work of Proshika in Bangladesh, CDRO in Guatemala and ORAP in Zimbabwe demonstrates with crystal clarity that participation, especially for the most marginalised people in a community, requires the establishment of complex multi-layered structures which enable decision-making to start at the lowest level possible.

Development researchers have observed that when NGOs work through existing power structures, it is very difficult for them to reach the powerless and that what is often referred to as "the empowerment of communities" would often more aptly be termed the "enrichment of individuals" [7]. As Benjamin Son Turnil, executive director of CDRO, points out, to avoid these pitfalls requires "the creation of new institutions...of community institutions".

Yet, while working through existing structures may simply reinforce inequalities and promote underdevelopment, ignoring or bypassing established power bases can cause great hostility which undermines or destroys the development process. What is required is a delicate and skilful balancing act, a feat which few organisations have accomplished.

Proshika, CDRO and ORAP have much in common in their approach to structures. The basic building block is the family unit. These come together in village groupings of people with a high degree of common interest. "It is in these groups that the poor engage themselves in the participatory planning of their development," says Dr Qazi Faruque Ahmed, the executive director of Proshika.

These groups then elect representatives on to the formal structure which forwards proposals to the centre and sets strategy for the structure as a whole. "People must participate in planning, monitoring and evaluation," says Sithembiso Nyoni, the chief executive of ORAP. These structures achieve a blend of collectivism and family-based activity which avoids the pitfalls of previous collective approaches.

Participation is a slow process, which is learned gradually: it has taken ORAP, Proshika and CDRO at least 10 years to arrive at where they are today. Conscious and constant efforts are needed to help people learn how to participate effectively [8]. But it is also important that there should be discernable success at an early stage in order to maintain people's confidence and interest in the activities in which they participate. In small ways, groups formed with the encouragement of the NGOs featured in this book did achieve rapid early success.

The result of effective participation is that people "own" their development, which thus becomes more sustainable. "We can do things on our own. We no longer beg. We are independent," says Elizabeth Ndlovu of the Zama Women's Garden Project in Zimbabwe. And Mohammed Abdul Hossain, a member of Maddha Jahangirabad Bhumihin Samity in Bangladesh, declares confidently: "We do not need loans any more. Even if Proshika withdraws from the village, we will be taking on new projects from...our own funds."

Communities

Communities are often referred to conveniently and incorrectly as homogeneous and harmonious units: all we need to do is listen to the "community" and all will be resolved. This is naive at best. Communities are subject to many forces and dynamics, and encompass a whole range of inequalities and inequities, which means that community development has to be a much more painstaking—and, at times, disjointed—exercise than is often assumed. There is always a wide range of views and perspectives, even—or perhaps especially—at the family level. One of the most striking differences is between men and women, and the case studies show repeatedly how important it is for women to have their own representative groups and structures.

Reactions to the very severe drought in Matabeleland, Zimbabwe, exemplify the wide range of opinions to be found in the same community, or similar communities. One woman, a group mobiliser, says: "We will dig the river banks. This happened in the last drought. Below those sands there is some water. So, together with all able-bodied men, we will dig." A

Communities are not homogenous entities but encompass a wide range of people, with varying views and interests.

common cry is for more boreholes, but some people, like 62-year-old Agnes Mtunzi, have lost faith in these: "Most of our pumps have broken down, and some boreholes have dried up."

The governor of the province of Matabeleland North has his own opinion: "Because of recurring droughts, water tables in most of Matabeleland have lowered. Most boreholes have not served adequately. Water programmes should concentrate on dam construction rather than borehole drilling." This view is supported by a government worker in Tsholotsho who says: "If there is a big dam, we can all grow and make big money."

Given all the differing views, it becomes extremely hard to decide which voices to listen to. Not only is it difficult to ensure that you are listening to the poorest, but you may then discover that they do not speak with a united voice either. Indeed, one effect of poverty and desperate circumstances can be to increase the disparity of views on solutions to problems.

A community's opinions of the "development expert"

● Much investigation and little action. "They show off with data."

● Very good at motivating people, but weak on carrying out the actions on a particular problem.

● They are not fluent in Quiche. They assess things in Spanish.

● They don't hear us, they don't listen to us, unless we pat them on the back.

● They constantly repeat that they love us, but we see the reality: they don't marry indigenous women. Indigenous women still carry out domestic work at home.

● They don't use medicinal plants, they don't dance to our tunes, they don't eat what we eat.

● They don't integrate themselves into our organisations.

● They want to be godparents, but they wouldn't choose us as their godparents.

● If we are sick, they don't visit us. They don't accompany us to burials, they don't grieve over what we grieve over.

● They prefer individual leadership, they forget collective leadership. For the most part their work does not have community support.

● They don't speak face to face in a systematic way. They only speak to the leader of the programme, but after that nothing.

● They don't know about our jokes, our stories, our beliefs, but they claim that they "know" us.

● They ask permission to come in, but not to leave. They go when they want. We don't have control over the programmes and projects, supervision or evaluation.

● Never have we participated in the selection of the experts, technicians and other professionals who say they are working with us.

Source: Cortes, C A, Hurtado, L, and Ortiz, V, *Breve Información Esquemática sobre el Proyecto de Comunicación Educativa con Poblaciones Nativas Tradicionales*, UNICEF, Guatemala, July 1990.

The development "expert"

It is easy for outsiders to visit a community and think that they have grasped very quickly what the problems are. The respect and deference with which they are treated in many communities may encourage them to believe in their own superior expertise, even their own infallibility.

Experience in Totonicapan, Guatemala, is salutary here. "All the projects which we had at that time were directed by institutions, and the communities were limited to receiving them without having the opportunity to express an opinion," remembers Son Turnil of CDRO. While these institutions were beginning to promote community participation, this was "not much more than a mere idea". The result was that the institutions usually took the lead and the participation of the community was reduced, in the best cases to a collaboration, while in the worst cases they simply translated their work into Quiche.

Son Turnil's evidence is corroborated by the peasants of Totonicapan. They remember development experts as "some strangers who came to chat to us with difficult words about what we needed, and who didn't listen to us. They went, and we again found ourselves alone with our sadnesses".

The box (opposite) expresses some of the views of Maya-Quiche people in Guatemala about the development "expert", but these are reactions which could well have been expressed by other communities who encounter "outsiders" eager to solve their problems. The criticisms demonstrate that intervention is highly suspect if it is not accompanied by humility, and a capacity to listen and learn. It is only over time that a community will come genuinely to trust and accept an outsider as a friend and equal and express to that person what their deepest feelings really are.

Beyond the project

Development is often dominated by the project—actions limited by time and sector, defined by target group and geographical area, and judged by pre-set objectives and yardsticks of success. This approach is often unsuitable for meeting the needs of communities, particularly poorer communities. If projects conceived by outsiders are seen as paramount they tend to stifle participation [9]. Instead of coming with preconceived ideas about the desirability of particular projects, development organisations need to support the establishment and smooth running of participative structures, and listen to the demands that arise from those structures.

Support needs clear "rules of engagement", so both sides know what is and is not acceptable within flexible boundaries. There are certain services that a development organisation may simply be unable or unwilling to provide. These rules should also describe what both sides expect out of the relationship. This should then form the basis for monitoring and evaluation.

Alleviating poverty

The professed aim of much development is to help the poorest people, although the reality of much official development assistance is clearly quite different. Even organisations which make strenuous and committed efforts to reach the poorest can find it difficult to translate their principles into action, as many evaluations have demonstrated [10]. First, there are genuine problems in identifying the poorest level of society. Second, if techniques to identify this sector are successful, there remains the difficulty of ensuring participation, as well as long-term support.

Perhaps this is inevitable: at the lowest stratum of society, the constraints on people's ability to organise are considerable. People may also be unwilling to be identified as the poorest of the poor: stigma is a powerful force in every community.

In the case studies in this book, the evidence of benefits to the poorest is somewhat mixed. FIDA in Uganda acknowledges that it has not been able to identify the poorest women and has therefore made its services available to women generally. But the testimony from Guatemala, Zimbabwe, India and Bangladesh would suggest that, at least to a certain extent, the poorest have benefited. Jamila Khatun, a landless woman in Bangladesh, says: "I am no longer haunted by dreams that the *jotdars* [large landowners] are forcing me out of my hut."

It is clear that JSK and its sister organisations PBKMS and SMS in West Bengal have reached and involved the poorest—landless agricultural labourers—but their record has been varied. Their mobilisation of *samities* (groups) has led to provision of specific services, such as tubewells. Alpana Das says: "We had been appealing for a tubewell.... Fed up, we *gheraoed* [surrounded] the officials with women carrying empty vessels. They had to give in and within two weeks they had arranged it." But their broader campaigns for better employment rights for the poor have yet to bear fruit.

The poor, and women in particular, are clearly benefiting in Guatemala as a result of CDRO's efforts. In a recent survey, 80% said that their health had improved, 78% that their social condition was better and 55% that their income had increased. The stories of Consuelo women's group and Transfrutas confirm this picture.

The Bangladesh case study suggests that the very poorest may have more chance of work when those a little less poor than themselves reclaim common land than when this land is illegally "owned" by the elite and often left unused. And so we may have to be brave enough to recognise two things. First, targeting the bottom 10% but missing the bottom 5% is far better than missing the bottom 10% altogether. There may even be a basis for arguing that between the poorest echelons of specific communities a "trickle-down" effect can be achieved.

Second, it is important to recognise that changes that seem negligible to outsiders may constitute a real benefit for those they affect, even if they simply raise self-confidence, or if they enable women to work a little less hard than before. Moreover, these improvements, small as they are, will not happen overnight, but will take years to reach fruition [11].

Women and development

Most of the studies in this book focus on women. This is not surprising, since women predominate in the poorest and most overworked segments of nearly every society.

For many women, full-time employment is impossible because of the burden of their domestic responsibilities. Indeed, time is such a constraint for women that without the introduction of labour-saving devices it is very difficult for them to benefit from income-generating programmes. Piped water or water tanks and fuel-efficient stoves would make a considerable difference to their daily lives, as would grinding machines for the preparation of food. Often, credit is not available for these items unless they form part of profit-making activities in their own right. Perhaps credit institutions need to take a broader look at the financing of labour-saving devices for women within the home.

Fresh approaches to organisation are needed so that women can fit in work around their new businesses, as one example from Guatemala makes clear: 50 women each working fours hours a week may be worth much more to the community, and be much more feasible for poorer women, than five women each working 40 hours. Attempts to promote nutrition and food security also need to recognise these time and work constraints, as is demonstrated in the case of small grain production in Zimbabwe.

Ensuring the active participation of women is not easy. All the case studies highlight gender bias within communities. Romelia Gutierrez of CDRO says: "The problem is that because the woman has always been in second position, today there are few communities where this has been overturned. *Machismo* [male supremacy] is always there in the culture. While a characteristic of our communities is organisation, within it female participation is not valued." Santa Martina García, a member of Consuelo women's group in Guatemala, complains: "When I say to my husband that I must go out he says: 'Hurry up then, get up early, do your jobs and then go out and don't be late.'" Similarly, Khodeja Begum in Bangladesh was prevented from joining a *samity* by her husband, who said that "NGOs corrupt ladies and...suck out money from the poor".

FIDA in Uganda and SMS in India work specifically with women and have achieved some measure of success. Other case studies show that without gender-specific programmes, it is much more difficult to achieve the equal involvement of women within participative structures.

Land rights

A theme that reappears again and again in the case studies is that of land rights. There are two aspects to this. First, there is the general issue of land reform, so that poor and landless people are given access to land. It is clear from numerous examples in this book that poor people want land from which to gain direct, productive advantage, such as farming or fishing rights.

Many land reform programmes have gone awry in the past: *ujamaa* in Tanzania and Soviet-inspired programmes in Ethiopia and eastern Europe were attempts to collectivise the land that were dictated by the state and foundered not least because they were imposed from above.

Bangladeshi law now makes *khas* or common land officially accessible to landless people, but enforcement lags behind the law. For landless women, *khas* land symbolises their freedom from serfdom. Kulsum Begum tells of a meeting held with the intention of wresting some *khas* land from *jotdars* (powerful landowners): "Seeing the big crowd of landless poor, I was no longer nervous and doubtful about our success. We told them one by one that the *khas* land was ours. The *jotdars* had been enjoying it for a long time, but now we wanted it. We threatened...that if they did not allow us into the *khas* land, we would use force." The *jotdars* gave way because they recognised that the women were "united and determined".

The second aspect concerns women's rights to land. In Bangladesh, a widow loses the right to her late husband's land. The *machista* (male-dominated) culture in Latin America militates against women acquiring land. In Zimbabwe and Uganda, women have no customary rights over land at all.

Talia Nansamba, a Ugandan woman, was effectively abandoned by her husband after seven years of marriage. He appointed a local male dignitary to administer his estate. "[This man] took over all the property, and sent me off the land which my husband had left for me. He told me never to dare set foot on the land or even harvest anything. I had a plantation full of food. My late co-wife's daughter was also chased off the land...We were helpless and desperate as we had nowhere to go."

It is clear that land rights and women's rights cannot be separated. "If you have a field of your own, you can use the money as you like, without anyone controlling you. You are not like a child," says Tenjiwe Moyo in Zimbabwe.

Work, employment and income

No individual or family can survive without an income, and the rising cost of such items as medicine, school fees and transport makes this all the more vital. In one survey in Zimbabwe, 69% of rural people identified income-generation or work as their first priority, while only 23% put social benefits from development first [12].

The studies in this book underline that people want a secure income, whether it comes from employment or self-employment. While many of the groups and individuals seem happy to become small entrepreneurs, there are those who would prefer to see the government create jobs. "If only the government could employ our men", says a member of the Zama Women's Garden Project in Zimbabwe.

Most of the NGOs in these case studies support income-generating activities by providing credit, training and advice. There has long been a reluctance, among NGOs in particular, to call these activities "businesses". Yet that is clearly what they are. The methods of organisation, operation and division of labour may vary from community to community, but it is clear that rural entrepreneurs, even those from the poorest sections of the community, seek to run sustainable, independent businesses. When this is achieved, it should be celebrated. Subsidised group activities are often much more comfortable for NGOs to live with, though sometimes their long-term success rate is poor and they often remain dependent on the supporting organisation.

Credit is usually the cornerstone of income-generating activities. Loans are relatively small, and the returns appear insignificant at first glance. A poultry-farming project in Chitax in Guatemala earns just US$14.28 a month. The members of the Purba Jahangirabad Bhumihin Samity in Bogra in Bangladesh earn up to US$50 a month each from their group activities. But the agricultural wage in Bangladesh can be as little as 25 US cents a day—under US$10 a month—and it is seasonal and uncertain. The annual income per capita in Totonicapan province in Guatemala is only US$50. Even earning enough money to pay for their children's school fees can make an enormous difference both to the morale of a family and to their future financial security. This is amply evidenced in the stories from women in Zimbabwe, Guatemala and Uganda.

Security is always a problem for credit-giving institutions, especially those working with the poorest, who have no collateral. The solution chosen by CDRO, ORAP and Proshika is that of collective guarantees: the group guarantees the loan to an individual member, taking responsibility for repaying it if for any reason he or she defaults. This arrangement has led to very high repayment rates, and works best where there are very homogeneous and strong groups. When CDRO moved out of its home area, it found that it could no longer rely on the group guarantee and needed a more formal contract.

While credit has a central role to play in the establishment and strengthening of income-generating activities, it is often not enough on its own. This is particularly true for poorer people who lack confidence and experience in running small businesses. For them, training and continued support are vital to ensure a success rate significant enough to encourage others down the same road.

Self-employment is a laudable goal, but is unable on its own to address the monetary needs of the entire population. Formal employment will continue to be the only feasible option for many people. The fundamental aim of PBKMS and its 20,000 members is to ensure work at all times for everyone. "The right to work is our birthright" is their motto. FIDA in Uganda recognises that its work on rights for women means little outside the context of access to productive resources, income and employment for women.

Sustainability

It is unlikely that any of the organisations featured in this book will achieve total financial self-sufficiency. More important is that they should achieve stability and be able to plan confidently for the long term. This requires a commitment and flexibility from donors to ensure that participative planning can be met with the right resources at the right time.

Ron Giling/Panos Pictures

Women labourers protesting. Organisations such as SMS in India have helped mobilise women to claim employment and land rights.

Sustainability is a concept that has at least three meanings, particularly in the eyes of donors. First, there is the question of whether the activities supported by a specific NGO are sustainable; that is, will they carry on in the long term? Ecological viability is clearly an important dimension of this, as are the economic and social factors which enable an activity to continue and flourish. This kind of sustainability also implies that the successful development NGO is the one which ultimately becomes redundant: when the development process becomes self-sustaining, there is no further need for external stimulus. This, for example, is CDRO's professed aim.

The evidence in this book is mixed: it appears that while all the NGOs have supported some activities which are fast moving towards sustainability and independence, none of them foresee a time when their work will no longer be needed. Proshika has probably made the greatest progress towards this goal.

The second issue concerns replicability. Some argue that unless initiatives can be copied by others, unless development pools spread out from their original boundaries, then development is not really sustainable.

Third, many local NGOs are expected to become self-sustaining in their own right—to operate a range of income-generating activities which provide them with the income they need to undertake their work without being reliant on external finance. Two problems arise here. First, NGOs can end up competing—often from a position of unfair advantage—with the very people they seek to support. Second, they are often not very good at running these activities (because their expertise lies elsewhere). These self-funding efforts can end up absorbing a lot of resources—both human and financial—and contribute little financially to the organisation.

CDRO now generates 75% of its funds through the sale of handicrafts, traditional medicines, vegetables, fruit juice and sweets. ORAP, too, is investing in a range of income-generating activities but is still largely dependent on donors. "As long as I cannot go to the treasury and ask for funds, I cannot see ourselves becoming donor-free," says ORAP's executive coordinator, Sithembiso Nyoni.

Scaling up

Much has been said over the last few years about scaling up and spreading the benefits of successful development activity. Yet the practical examples are few. Scaling up cannot take place without the involvement of governments—indeed many would argue that it should not happen without government intervention. There are few NGOs which would present themselves as long-term alternatives to government or the private sector as providers of services.

There is a need for greater coordination between local NGOs, governments and international organisations, but relations between these are often characterised by tension, as the case studies show. In Guatemala, for example, the governor of Totonicapan, Rolando García, says: "My criticism, or let us say my call, is for...CDRO to work closely with government institutions, so that our work is coordinated and we are not working on different sides. Disordered work brings no benefits."

A similar complaint is made against ORAP by Zimbabwean government officials: "All other NGOs such as the Freedom from Hunger Campaign, the Catholics and Oxfam first come and talk to us, but ORAP just goes straight to the villagers." Mohammed Abdul Kader, general secretary of Singair Thana Jatiya Party (the third largest opposition party in Bangladesh) complains: "We are politically antagonistic to NGOs because we see them as the new East India Company." But he sees Proshika as an exception, praising the organisation for "giving new life to the poor".

Clearly the scaling up of participative structures needs the full support of government. International organisations have a powerful role to play in encouraging bureaucrats to embrace participation as a means of improving their effectiveness and, indeed, in the long run, making their lives easier.

Social services

The governments of many countries have reduced their support to basic social services over the last decade, often as a direct result of structural adjustment programmes. While many of the organisations covered in this study have, to some extent, stepped in to fill the gaps as they have opened up, it is clear that people still expect governments to provide a range of social services. "If it's a people's government," protests one Zimbabwean woman, "how can they reintroduce hospital and school fees?"

Drinking water, sanitation, housing, roads, communications, health and education are all clear priorities for rural communities, and the scope of individual NGOs will never be wide enough to embrace whole populations; nor, arguably, would it be appropriate for them to operate on such a vast scale. It is dangerous to assume that the private sector will ever be able to meet these needs either, while the purchasing power of rural communities is so low.

Food security

It is fundamental to any development programme that people have enough to eat, and that they have the security of knowing where their next meal will come from. Most of all, they need to have the energy and physical strength to engage in the activities which can enhance the quality of their lives. The means of ensuring food security are clear: better storage, better distribution, more drought-resistant crops, more irrigation. But the practice is much more difficult.

Often, food supplies are attacked from a number of different directions at the same time. "As if the lack of rains were not enough, mice ate up the little food there was and frost wiped out all the vegetables," says Zimbabwean Jeremiah Langa, who complains that his appeals to the government have gone unanswered.

Food security can be improved through reducing pre- and post-harvest losses, and through better crop storage and distribution, but ultimately genuine food security can be achieved only through poverty alleviation, so that people can afford to buy food when they need it. There can be no long-term security while, in the words of Rukeya Begum in West Bengal, "we can't afford to eat the rice we grow".

The tendency for food to be "pigeon-holed" as part of emergency provision tends to overshadow the need for food security as part of long-term development activity. Yet it is often the case that until a community has enough to eat it is unable to participate effectively in any development process.

Emerging from crisis

The issue of food security is one illustration among many of the need to address the continuum between emergency and development work, so that relief provision in times of disaster protects and strengthens—rather than undermining—long-term development efforts. Equally, giving priority to social development—in the areas identified by poor people themselves as the most crucial to their wellbeing—is perhaps the single most effective way of helping to build a capacity for disaster preparedness, and even of preventing disaster in the first place.

As emphasised at the beginning of this chapter, social development cannot simply be left to communities and the organisations that support them. Action at national and international level needs to complement local action, and rhetoric needs to be backed up with resources.

Simon Burne

From the Roots to the Sky

Culture, participation and development in Guatemala

Guatemala's civil war, which reached its peak in the 1980s, left the impoverished Maya-Quiche people of rural Totonicapan even more marginalised than before. **Fabiana Frayssinet** reports on the successful efforts of CDRO (Association for Cooperation and the Rural Development of Western Guatemala) to help the community cross the poverty threshold—through development programmes based on the principles of Maya-Quiche culture— and on the difficulties of scaling up such activities. Photographs by **Luis Ascui**.

Oh you, Heart of the Sky and Heart of the Earth!
Turn towards us your glory and your riches.
Give life and development to my children! [1]

Long ago, the tribes of the prosperous Maya-Quiche kingdom were already practising what the development experts of today are preaching: sustainable human development. Care for the earth and its resources was integral to their culture and in accordance with the most sacred principles of their cosmic vision.

This philosophy guides the work of the Associación para la Cooperación y el Desarrollo Rural de Occidente (Association for Cooperation and the Rural Development of Western Guatemala) (CDRO). "The world is not a store of independent resources unrelated to human life," CDRO has stated. "On the contrary, it is a vital part of development and life in general.... We are within the world, not outside it. If we damage it, it will damage us; if we exploit it excessively, without seeking equilibrium, if we don't put back what we take, we are preparing our own death and the death of the other species which carry out an essential function in the maintenance of life [2]".

Laureano García Axocom, the leader of a Maya-Quiche commune in the western province of Totonicapan, points out that these ideas have been handed down from generation to generation. "Yesterday, I had the opportunity to listen to Cuban and Chilean scientists, agricultural technology experts in organic cultivation," he says. "I admire the depth of their science, but in reality the only thing they did was to give scientific support to what we, the Mayas, have been doing for millennia."

Guatemala in crisis

During the 1980s, Guatemala's violent 30-year conflict between the army and left-wing guerrillas reached its peak, resulting in the deaths of more than 150,000 people. As a result of the violent conflict, 15% of women are widows [3].

With a population of over 9 million, Guatemala ranks 103rd out of the 173 developing countries on the Human Development Index of the United Nations Development Programme [4]. According to the United Nations Children Fund (UNICEF), 85% of the population are poor and 66% live in absolute poverty; 6.1 million people have no access to drinking water and 3.9 million lack adequate sanitation; 500,000 children under five are malnourished, and 1.4 million children receive no education [5].

Although Guatemala subscribes to the United Nations Protocol on Economic, Social and Cultural Rights, violations of all these rights form part of daily life according to the Archbishop's Office for Human Rights [6]. Sixty-five per cent of the population are unemployed and 57% are illiterate. Nearly three-quarters of the land is owned by just 2% of the population, and the monthly minimum wage of 1,764 quetzals (US$63) does not cover the cost of a basket of basic goods for a month for a typical family (currently estimated to be US$219).

The indigenous Mayan people, whose 23 ethnic groups together comprise 60% of the population, are living through one of the most difficult periods of their history. The "lost decade" of the 1980s left them further marginalised, but the process which impoverished a once prosperous people began 500 years ago. CDRO has no doubts about the origin of the Mayan people's hardship: "It is clear that the current conditions are a consequence of the historic process of colonisation, which, as it affected the ancient organisational structures of the Maya-Quiche, led to a severe loss of control over survival strategies, management of resources and understanding of the process of change [7]."

Similarly, the Assembly of Civil Society, held in Guatemala City in July 1994, referred to a system of permanent domination since the Spanish invasion, "which has brought about conditions of extreme poverty, destitution, plunder, marginalisation and oppression of the Mayas, denying them the exercise of their rights to maintain their identity, and to possess the territorial and environmental sustenance they need [8]".

The Assembly was held as a result of the peace dialogue between government and guerrillas. It concluded that real peace would not be possible unless conditions were established for a just, democratic and plural state and society, with the direct participation of the Mayan people.

There is a chance, therefore, for the revival of the Mayan cosmic vision.

Poverty in Totonicapan

And their hearts were afflicted, and they were suffering greatly: they had no food, they had no sustenance. But they only had to smell the points of their walking sticks to feel satisfied [9].

Even poorer than the rest of Guatemala, the province of Totonicapan is a remote, mountainous region of 1,061 sq km, inhabited by fewer than 330,000 people. Indigenous Maya-Quiche people form 97.5% of its population. Of the total population, 87.5% live in rural areas, and 88% are poor [10]. The rate of illiteracy is 41.8%. Only 33.7% of homes have a water supply and

31% have some form of sanitation. These figures are reflected in the low level of life expectancy (54 years) and high rates of infant mortality (73.4 for every 1,000 live births).

Incomes are very low: an average of 1,400 quetzals (US$50) per year in the rural areas and 3,220 quetzals (US$115) in the urban areas. The principal productive activity of the region is handicraft, but this is heavily reliant on middlemen and thus scarcely profitable. Rural people combine artisinal production with smallholder agriculture on poor soils. The basic diet is maize, rice, beans, pulses, herbs, vegetables and greens: the consumption of meat is a privilege reserved for festive or market days.

"Alone again with our sadnesses"

In April 1981, a group of leaders of various villages from Xolsacmalja and Nimasac met to discuss the situation of the people of Totonicapan and why they had been failed by development organisations.

"All the projects which we had at that time were directed by outside organisations, and the communities were limited to accepting them without having the opportunity to express an opinion," remembers Benjamin Son Turnil, the executive director of CDRO.

Various national and international organisations had begun to promote community participation, but it "was not much more than a mere idea", according to Son Turnil. Usually, the institutions took the lead, restricting community participation to—at best—collaboration in implementing projects. "In the worst cases, all they did was to translate their work into Quiche. Sometimes the dogs would chase away these 'experts' when they visited our communities."

The evidence of Son Turnil is corroborated by the peasants of Totonicapan. A group of men sit at the roadside, winding hanks of thread which they will later weave into cloth. Recalling their experience of past development projects, Juan Ixtaj speaks of "some strangers who came to chat to us with difficult words about what we needed, and who didn't listen to us". He sighs. "They went, and we again found ourselves alone with our sadnesses."

CDRO is born

Then they arrived at the summit of a mountain, and there all the Quiche people and tribes met. There they held council to make their arrangements [11].

The village leaders decided to establish an organisation which would be guided by the principles of Maya-Quiche culture, promoting community participation to energise social development.

In 1984, with an initial grant from USAID, CDRO began its work. The organisation is now integrated into some 30 rural communities in Totonicapan, operating through 400 groups which together benefit, directly or indirectly, some 40,000 rural people.

CDRO describes itself as a channel through which organised communities express their interests and carry out their work according to their own cultural values, using available science and technology. It is committed to "total participation", maintaining that a programme of development is worthless unless it is under the direct control of the community. To ensure this degree of participation, CDRO has established a three-tiered organisational structure, called Pop, consisting of Grassroots Groups, the Community Council and the General Assembly.

Grassroots Groups are made up of people united by a common interest and with a plan of work. The Grassroots Groups of each community are represented on the Community Council. Each Community Council is then represented in the General Assembly, the highest authority in the organisation. In addition, CDRO has created Subsystems which bring together all the groups of the same type. There are eight of these, representing artisans, farmers, women, health promoters, consumer cooperatives and groups involved in infrastructure improvement, social services, education and capacity-building. These, in western terms, are the sectoral programmes of the institution.

The principle of community participation is visible at every level of CDRO's organisation, including at its headquarters. Housed in a modern building in the chief town of the province, all the employees there, many of them dressed in strictly

Poultry production is one of the income-generating activities supported by CDRO that benefits Maya-Quiche women.

traditional dress and speaking perfectly both Spanish and Quiche, were recruited from the same communities with their recommendation. "My neighbours elected me to the council", explains Maria, coordinator of the women's artisanal programme, who, like other CDRO workers, has had to get to grips with the odd world of "project work".

Reflecting on the reasons for the success of CDRO, Son Turnil attributes its achievements to the use of culture as a resource to promote social change.

"There have been many indigenous movements which turn things upside down, claiming that only the past has any value. We try and blend the past with the present," he explains. "Without rejecting the achievements of the past we are trying to confront modern problems, always within our cultural framework. For example, to raise the consciousness of a community, we could use the method of Paulo Freire [the popular education expert from Brazil], but this wouldn't work for us. For us, what makes community consciousness-raising easier, is to analyse with them their history, their own Maya-Quiche history, and through that we discover together so many valuable elements of our culture. We want to arrive at this collective memory which the Maya-Quiche people preserve, and when we get there, that is when we have succeeded."

Credit and solidarity

They spoke, consulting each other and meditating. They reached agreement, joined their words and their thoughts [12].

To promote sustainability and self-reliance, CDRO gives priority to productive projects that can be financed through loans. However, it does also give grants, seeing these as a way of encouraging communities to get closer to the organisation and to build confidence, so that later they can become involved in productive projects. An example of such a progression can be seen in the activities of a women's group in Xantun, which approached CDRO for a donation for improving housing, and which later went into the production of sweet bread and *atol* (a protein-rich cereal for children), assisted by a CDRO loan.

There is a 98% repayment record on loans, far higher than that of many other credit organisations. Son Turnil connects this with the same "system of solidarity and mutual support" which governs all community activities. "Credit is granted to the community who asks for it," he says. "If the group has any difficulty in repaying, it is the community who sorts things out. It is the community who puts pressure on to repay the loan or helps out if necessary. Sometimes the communities use other ways to guarantee the repayment of credit, but the preference is for the system of mutual support, which is a social system, not a mortgage system."

The solidarity that forms the basis of social and economic relations is in evidence in the most remote communities in Totonicapan. After taking a twisting road up into the mountains, passing through hundreds of maize fields and kitchen gardens, we arrive at the hamlet of Chitax which, from its lofty position, looks down over most of the cultivated land of the region.

In one of the houses, a group of indigenous women are talking animatedly about a loan which CDRO has given them to improve their poultry production. Their children listen to the conversation while doing domestic chores, learning from their mothers the first steps in community organisation. The conversation stops when we arrive, and with the courtesy and formality of their traditional culture, they make room for us to sit beside them and explain the reasons for our visit.

With the help of a translator, Paula Tax, one of the group's leaders, whom her colleagues respectfully allow to speak, explains that they are meeting "to discuss the loan, to see how much money we are going to repay to CDRO". These women have known each other for a long time, meeting frequently when going to the market to sell their products, collecting water or transporting wool. Today they sit together, united and strengthened around a common interest because, insists Juana, "the same poverty made us unite all the more".

Credit, although acquired collectively, may be used for individuals, according to their needs. One woman explains that she used it to buy more pigs and hens. Another says she spent the money on vaccines, "because all the chickens were dying". Yet

Loans are given to groups who may distribute them to individuals to use according to their own priorities.

another used it to fatten her cow and pigs.

The loans are provided by the Pop Bank, the institution which manages the resources of the Subsystems, the Councils and the Grassroots Groups and encourages savings and productive activities. The interest rate charged is much lower than the general bank rate. To compensate for this, the bank charges very high rates to individuals or to people outside CDRO.

Women and *machismo*

The meat of man is made from maize, but when woman was wrought by the Creator and Former, her meat was made from reeds. The Creator and Former wished that these materials be used in their composition [13].

Within Mayan culture, women traditionally played the role of educators and communicators and were actively involved in the maintenance and development of the Mayan identity. Maya-Quiche culture originally gave women a position of great importance. It was women who first cultivated and improved maize, giving rise to a civilisation based on agriculture [14].

But exposure to Latin *machista* (male-dominated) culture has led to women being relegated to a secondary role. Indigenous leaders such as Rosalina Tuycuc, of the National Coordinating Committee for Widows of Guatemala, traces this change to the recruitment of indigenous men into the army, where "cultural values are deformed and they are taught to consider women inferior".

The marginalisation of women in formal productive activities derives in great part from their lack of education. Guatemala is the Latin American country with the highest level of female illiteracy. Among Maya women illiteracy is nearly three times higher than it is among non-indigenous women: 71.9% compared to 24.6%. Of the total Guatemalan adult female population, some 1.4 million have not had one year of formal education.

In this context, CDRO has been running since 1988 a Programme for the Promotion of Women (*Joju Nam*) which has so far succeeded in organising 45 groups in 25 associated communities, representing some 1,500 women. The groups work in seven programme Subsystems: handicrafts—producing ribbons, traditional bags, sandals embroidered by machine, and yellow and black soap; infrastructure—improving housing, installing grills and gas stoves; agriculture—caring for and maintaining laying hens, pigs and bulls, and cultivating communal and family kitchen gardens; education and capacity-building; production—running a fruit-drying plant and a grain mill; consumer cooperatives; and training in health and nutrition.

"Now we can do everything"

Their wives were there when they woke up, and at that moment their hearts filled with joy because of their wives [15].

A meeting of the Consuelo women's group in Xantun is under way. Consuelo (which means 'solace') has 24 members and demonstrates clearly what can be achieved with both motivation and opportunity. Considered by Candelaria Perez, CDRO's women's group coordinator, to be one of the most dynamic groups, the women of Xantun started their relationship with CDRO with a programme of grill installation, kitchen improvement, making of *atol,* and health education. Initially, CDRO gave them a loan of 35,000 quetzals (US$1,250) to be repaid over two years. Divided among the 28 women, this represented 52 quetzals (US$1.86) a month for each woman.

The group has just embarked on a bread-making initiative. With the good humour that characterises Maya-Quiche women despite their heavy social responsibilities, the women continue to mix and knead the dough while participating in the meeting.

Asked if these groups, unaccustomed to handling credit, have fears about getting into debt, Candelaria explains: "The point is that credit is given to groups which already have a productive activity. If they don't have one, they start one. When we give a loan, we are near the communities in order to support them in their projects."

The women take turns twice a week to produce the bread, which is then sold in the city because "today it is not like before when we stayed at home out of pure necessity," explains Sebatiana Tatiac, one of the group's members. "Now we know how to do everything, just imagine, and we help our husbands with groceries, clothing and medicines."

But despite the increase in household income, the women of Consuelo group admit that their production is less than it might be because of restrictions placed on them by the men. "When I say to my husband that I must go out, he says: 'Hurry up then, get up early, do your jobs and then go out and don't be late,'" says Santa Martina García. The limitations imposed by men's attitudes are mentioned by all the women's groups visited.

"The problem is that because the woman has always been in second position, today there are few communities where this has been overturned. *Machismo* [male supremacy] is always there in the culture. While a characteristic of our communities is organisation, within it female participation is not valued," explains Romelia Gutierrez, coordinator of the poultry programme.

One of the objectives of CDRO's women's programme is to "raise awareness that the woman is complementary to the man".

1.4 million children in Guatemala receive no education. When a family has an adequate income the children are more likely to go to school.

To this end, it aims to improve the health of women, make them literate and build up their skills in production and selling. With the extra income resulting from successful productive activities, many women have started or completed their education, or at least have provided education for their daughters. "I tell you to look at my daughter, because I couldn't even get one year at school and today I can't read or write anything," says Micaela Tix, president of the women's handicraft group in Chiyax.

Micaela received a loan to increase the capital in her small business of making traditional clothes. "God helped us and CDRO gave us this capital. With the money, I bought material and sewing machines. Now I have a total of seven people working for me, three more than before." From her sales of trousers, shirts, waistcoats and other garments, she earns some 2,996 quetzals (US$107) a month. The money Micaela earns has brought a substantial improvement in her family's quality of life.

She tells us that her husband, also involved in the prosperous business, "doesn't go out any more to work on the *milpa* [maize smallholding]".

Fifteen-year-old Florinda Yax, whose family has a handloom-weaving business, also points out the advantages of credit. "We asked CDRO for credit because, before, I worked as an operative and I didn't earn much. Now we have two looms and we work with my father who in turn was instructed by my grandfather, and he by his father. Now we live solely by this and when I finish I'm going to study. I'm going to do my Second Basic [second level of primary education]." Florinda stops winding thread on the loom and collects her things to go to school.

Crossing the poverty line

CDRO's initial goal for all the projects it supports is to raise the living standards of participants from "the level of extreme poverty" and then to cross the poverty threshold. In simple terms, CDRO defines poverty as "when income is not sufficient to pay for food". "Last year we did an evaluation," says Son Turnil. "One of the indicators of when the poverty level has been passed is when families start to have a small capacity to save, because this indicates that they have overcome their principle problems. That was the intention and we have achieved it at least in part." But he says that national economic policy can be a constraint when, for example, there is a substantial hike in the price of basic commodities.

Despite these constraints, women involved with CDRO say that they have achieved improvements in food, medicine and clothes [16]. In Chitax, for example, a women's group applied to CDRO for a loan to enable them to bring electricity to their homes. Subsequently, they took out another loan, for animal husbandry activities, including poultry farming, which enabled them to increase their stock of animals and birds. Besides providing a more nutritious household diet, the women have been able to sell surplus products in the market. They report that this brings in an additional 400 quetzals (US$14.28) a month. In this region of extreme poverty, such a figure represents a significant improvement in the household economy.

The Chitax group is enthusiastic. "Now we sell eggs in the market because the hens are laying more.... We no longer have to buy eggs. Instead, we are selling them," says Santa Cruz Itax, a member of the group.

The improvement in quality of life that a loan can bring over time is described by Benita Antonia Vasquez, another member of the group: "The loan has benefited us enormously. I took out a loan and for two years I fattened livestock, feeding two cows, and with the money from the first of these I repaid part of the debt in the first year. With the second animal I succeeded in repaying all the debt and, with the money that I have earned since, I have bought a pig. Now I can sell milk and I have food for the family." As Benita tells her story, the other women in the group nod their heads in agreement.

Romelia Gutierrez explains that women who already keep hens for domestic use want to gain expertise with looking after laying birds which can bring them an income. "They receive courses in husbandry, hygiene and feeding, vaccination and the diseases which afflict birds," she says.

Small industry projects are another means by which women have been able to improve their lives. One of these, run by women from the villages of Xolsacmalja and Chuculjuyup, is a fruit-drying company called Transfrutas. Each family had about a dozen fruit trees, mostly apples and peaches, and the women were aware that much of the fruit was being left to rot in the sun. After watching a solar-drying demonstration, which convinced them that dried fruit kept all its flavour and nutritional value instead of staying "all wrinkled up there in the trees", they decided to start a fruit-drying business.

Today they are the owners of a drying plant which they take turns to operate so that other tasks are not neglected. They use an artificial method of drying, a small tray drier which is much more effective than the solar drier they had seen demonstrated. The drying process "is based on heating these trays," explains Simeona, a leader of the group, as she works. "We cut the fruit into little pieces and wait seven hours for it to dry." Types of fruit dried now include mango, pineapple and papaya.

The women earn much more than they did from the sale of

Transfrutas, a fruit-drying company run by women, is one of the most successful small industry projects in Totonicapan.

fresh apples. From profits made so far, they have repaid their CDRO loan. Future profits will go to increase the capital of the business which currently consists only of the tray drier and a fruit corer and peeler. Demand, too, is increasing. "Some German women came and wanted to buy two tonnes of dried mango from us," Simeona announces proudly. "So we will have to buy more equipment." Meanwhile, with the help of another plant with surplus capacity, the women will make a profit of 224,980 quetzals (US$8,035) on the sale. "[With this] we shall double our production capacity, improve our homes and have our own premises", the women enthuse.

It is a preoccupation of the managers of Transfrutas not to damage nature. "So we don't harm our neighbours", the women constructed a tank for the disposal of the liquid residues of the dried fruits.

Women breaking barriers

*Let the people have peace, much peace and may they be happy, and
give us a good life and a useful existence.... Grandfather of the Sun,
Grandfather of the Light, let the Dawn come [17].*

"They say that women can't take decisions without men, but this
is a lie. We tell women that they can also bring their ideas and
now we see that they are participating, asking their questions and
speaking out. Before, they were afraid to speak," says Romelia
Gutierrez. She herself initially had as many disadvantages as any
woman, but now she has completed her secondary studies and
intends to go to university.

Overcoming   the   barriers   of   written   and   spoken
communication, women are beginning to feel that they are the
managers of their own development. "Despite the constraints that
women face, the CDRO women's groups are succeeding bit by bit
in breaking these barriers, and already some of them have set up
their own businesses," explains Maria, a women's group
coordinator.

A study recently carried out by CDRO shows that women
have also benefited from other CDRO programmes. Eighty per
cent of the women responded that their own and their family's
level of health had improved. They attribute this to the home
improvement programme, use of medicinal plants and a more
nutritious diet. Improvements in social conditions were
mentioned by 78% of the women. These included drinking water
projects, home improvements, construction of—or improvements
to—schools, and the paving of roads [18].

Women unanimously felt that they had increased their
educational level. Reading and writing, self-expression,
organisational skills and knowledge of health matters had all
improved through the education, health and natural medicine
programmes [19].

The percentage reporting benefits from productive projects
was rather lower, although still significant: 55% said that their
income had increased and that they now had better food and
clothes. Still having a very low family income, women see the
next steps in their development as increasing their capacity to

undertake more productive work, increasing their capital, improving their products and extending the market for their products.

"Women's needs remain at a very basic level: improving housing, family income, health (nutrition and hygiene)," concludes the study.

Finding the way forward

May the existence be good of those who give you sustenance and food in your mouth, in your presence, to you, Heart of the Sky, Heart of the Earth [20].

There are many differing views within the community as to where the future development of the people lies.

Raymundo Say stresses the importance of education. "Our standard of living should be raised by putting more children in school. Without education, no one will ever escape from this blindness, because illiteracy is blindness," he asserts. Equally important to him is Maya-Quiche culture. "Our culture is part of our treasure. Most of us here in Guatemala are indigenous people...I wish that our culture could be respected, and our traditional dress."

For Basilio Chioc, who lives off the land, development is above all about access to education. "I couldn't study. I only reached Grade Three in primary school. I don't want my children to end up like me. You know that we peasants are good at making babies! I have 11 children by my wife, and I have only been able to put two into education...I want my children to improve their standard of living through learning."

Nonetheless, Basilio sees agriculture as the only means of survival for himself. "My other option would be business, exploiting the other poor people, but I couldn't in all conscience do that. So I worked hard to buy a small field, then I bought two bigger blocks of land which I still own today," he explains. Jesus Tax, another peasant farmer, thinks that while agriculture is "part of peasant life...we are going to have to look for alternatives, like small-scale agro-industry. We are just going to have to keep on asking our government [to develop this]."

While washing her clothes in the stream, Rosa Puac says that her greatest wish for her family is "to have money to buy medicines". A mother of seven, Rosa has had three miscarriages. One child died at the age of one, of a "stomach complaint".

Son Turnil expresses his own view: "Agriculture does not represent development for us; however, we work in agriculture. We work in handicrafts, but we also know that this does not represent for us alternative development. We support consumer cooperatives, but we know that they are very dependent on private business, and the same goes for other areas. Then why do we work in these areas? Because we are still at the stage of learning to manage the organisation. With the small resources that there are, we have to learn everything about total development."

He sees the forest as a major untapped resource but believes it should only be exploited within the Mayan framework of sustainable development. "In Totonicapan we have one of the richest forest reserves in the country. A field of trees is worth 10 or 12 times more than a field of maize. We estimate this forest resource to be worth 11.5 million quetzals (US$410,000), and that is without exhausting it. We think that this is where our development lies."

Son Turnil feels that agro-industry may also be a significant option but warns against the temptation to scale up some of the successful agro-industries such as Transfrutas, despite the fact that donors would be happy to provide finance. Transfrutas is at present only using 5% of available fruits, although there have been proposals to increase this to 10% and to convert the artisanal plant into a factory. But Son Turnil has reservations about such steps.

"The problem is to leave the communities with their own projects. If we were doing a real project, with a project mentality, carrying out a financial evaluation of the project, we would be faced with the real danger of losing the project. Because to scale up we would need managers, qualified people, people who don't exist within these communities. We would turn the project into a body foreign to the community, and that is not the idea."

Trying to take root

Let them not fall as the road rises and falls. Let them find obstacles neither behind nor in front of them, nor anything that will beat them [21].

CDRO recognises that for the moment it needs international assistance in order to consolidate and strengthen its work. However, its aim is to avoid dependency by establishing a range of self-managed and self-sufficient activities. Three-quarters of its funds are now self-generated, the balance coming from 17 external institutions. "We can't yet sustain ourselves totally but we can do it partially, through projects which are already under way, like handicrafts, which bring in a good return," declares Son Turnil.

The handicrafts programme, one of the pioneer programmes of CDRO, was created with the aim of supporting the work of artisans in the areas of organisation, production, capacity-building, credit and improving profits [22].

Today, the programme, which has 40 groups with a total membership of 700, has its own storehouse from which it is selling increasing numbers of products both inside the country and abroad. Commercial products include a wide range of traditional cloth, embroidered clothes and accessories. To improve the quality of the products by increasing control over critical parts of the process, a dye house and manufacturing centre was set up. Between July 1993 and June 1994, the programme had a turnover of 4 million quetzals (US$142,857), including exports worth 896,000 quetzals (US$32,000).

The natural medicine programme tries to improve health by using existing resources in the communities and reviving the use of natural or Mayan medicine. The programme promotes a consciousness within communities of the beneficial properties of natural medicine in curing common ailments, with very good results [23].

"We are trying to help the poor and also to promote faith in natural medicine. Manufactured drugs are more expensive and often produce other illnesses," says Juan Hermegildo Barreno, the programme's coordinator. "A drug treatment for amoebas comes

Juan Hermegildo Barreno, coordinator of the natural medicine programme, examines his medicinal herbs.

to 175 quetzals [US$6.25], but it only gives relief and won't get rid of the disease. In contrast, herbal remedies are natural, economic, they work and they only cost 73 quetzals [US$2.6] a treatment . People's health has improved one hundred per cent," he asserts.

The question of self-sufficiency and sustainability is valid not only for CDRO but also for each member community. "One of our objectives is...that CDRO will not be here all our lives. We have made people aware that the objective of CDRO is that they know how to work, know how to develop and carry out projects on their own if we ever pull out," says Candelaria. "What we want to achieve is that the community reaches a level of self-management—administering,   controlling   and   executing projects. This has to a great extent been achieved."

Some people working in development have expressed doubts about CDRO's effective coordination with other agencies. Rolando García, governor of Totonicapan, says: "My criticism, or let us say my call, is...for CDRO to work closely with government institutions, so that our work is coordinated and we are not working on different sides. Disordered work brings no benefits." He points out that the decentralisation plan which the government of Ramiro de León sees as crucial "to beat poverty" is being implemented in Totonicapan as a priority area, so that CDRO has a natural role to play [24].

"It is much more economical", he asserts, "and much more human to work from the grassroots upwards than to try to remedy a situation from the top down. It is better to tackle the fundamental causes of human insecurity, rather than its tragic consequences."

Despite his doubts, the governor recognises CDRO as the most important organisation in the Totonicapan area, and says that he shares with the head of the National Peace Foundation, Alvaro Colom, an admiration for this organisation. In García's view, CDRO contributes through three "key aspects" to the alleviation of the conditions of extreme poverty which affect the province: first, its ability to motivate communities; second, capacity-building ("now in Totonicapan we are authorising countless grassroots committees formed as a result of CDRO's efforts"); and third, project execution. In this context, he mentions an education project, now self-sustaining, which was supported by CDRO and which is now "an important engine of cultural development".

Spreading the word

Let them multiply and grow...those who call on you in the ravines, under the trees, under the lianas [25].

Could an experience such as CDRO's, which bases development alternatives in the Maya-Quiche culture, be applied in other communities in the country or in other countries? Is Maya fundamentalism, based on solidarity, communal participation and a sustainable relationship with nature, the unique key for success for this sort of management?

Son Turnil says it is not unusual to find similar organisations in other countries with large indigenous populations, such as Bolivia and Peru. He believes this is because all indigenous Latin American peoples have a shared tradition of collective work. However, where the culture is more heterogeneous, the CDRO director sees constraints in applying this organisational system. His doubts come from the experience of trying to extend the model to other parts of Guatemala.

Since 1988, CDRO has begun appraising and supporting other communities outside the province of Totonicapan. This has led to the formation of the Coordinating Committee of Integrated Development Associations in the Southwest of Guatemala (CADISOGUA), which brings together some 150 rural communities. In these—some of Mayan origin but "westernised" by migration—the recovery of loans, which depends on a culture of solidarity, is "more difficult", Son Turnil confirms. "Although many people are indigenous, they don't have a community life any more. Their culture has suffered a very great blow, and therefore a loan can't be given in the same way. A document is required—some land title deeds, or other papers to ensure the recovery of the loan."

Another limitation is that CDRO was established in an area characterised by the widespread distribution and ownership of smallholdings, with no large landowners. "It is very difficult to promote this same model of development in places where there are large estates because people are very tied to an agricultural enterprise which limits their community participation," explains Son Turnil. "In Totonicapan there are only small farmers. Because of this, they can participate in collective activities without having to ask anyone's permission."

Despite these constraints, CDRO is committed to seeing its work grow, believing as it does in the wisdom of the ancient Mayan people: "Let no one, neither one nor two of us, stay behind the others [26]".

Taking on the Powerful

Struggles of rural organisations in India

The plight of rural people in West Bengal, India, led to the establishment of JSK (the Centre for People's Solidarity). JSK subsequently helped to form PBKMS (the West Bengal Agricultural Labourers' Association), a mass organisation of the agricultural poor, and SMS, a parallel organisation for women labourers. As **Ranjita Biswas** discovers, people mobilised by these organisations are increasingly demanding justice, particularly in the area of land rights and employment. Photographs by **Kishor Roychowdhury**.

Milonmore is only about 120 km from Calcutta, the capital of West Bengal state in eastern India. But as our car bumps and struggles through the giant-sized potholes in the road, it seems as if we are going to another country. The lashing monsoon rain blurs our vision. While I am wondering what must be the state of the *kacha* (dirt) roads in the villages with such an onslaught of rain, I see to my astonishment a cycle-van (a cycle with a rough wooden seat for passengers) struggling through the fierce wind and rain. The passengers have only *gamchas* (cotton towels) to cover their heads. Perhaps someone has an umbrella, but that would be useless to hold off the torrent.

In West Bengal villages, these cycle-vans are the most widely-used form of transport. They carry people to the *haat* (weekly bazaar) or to visit relatives, and they even take sick people, or women in the throes of labour, to the distant health centre. Small wonder that some do not survive the journey.

We arrive finally at the Milonmore Centre of Paschim Banga Khet Majoor Samity (PBKMS) (West Bengal Agricultural Labourers' Association). This is a two-room building by the roadside, inconspicuous but for the board outside proudly proclaiming "Kajer adhikaar janmogoto adhikaar" ("The right to work is our birthright"). But when I meet Swapna Triparthy, Tahamina Begum and Shaktipada Bar, all in their mid- or early 20s, and listen to them talking enthusiastically of their plans to improve the lot of poor agricultural workers, I am suddenly made aware of a confidence seldom found in villagers.

Swapna is a dedicated worker in Shramjeevi Mahila Samity (SMS) (Women Labourers' Association), the women's equivalent of PBKMS. She has braved social ostracisation by daring to live in a commune along with male workers while still unmarried. Tahamina has broken out from a conservative Muslim background to work for the organisation. Shaktipada is another full-time activist. The Milonmore Centre has seven full-time workers in all, and serving 38 villages, it is one of the busiest centres run by PBKMS.

At another location, this time north of Calcutta, in the village of Maheswarpur, Badu District, about 40 km from the centre of power, there is a different scene. On the floor of a large, open-sided hall, men and women of different ages sit in a circle. They have papers and pencils to scribble notes on and lots of questions to ask. A workshop is taking place on the implications for poor indigenous farmers of the GATT (General Agreement on Tariffs and Trade) agreement which India has just signed. The venue is the *ashram* (centre for learning), as they like to call it, of Jana Sanghati Kendra (JSK) (Centre for People's Solidarity), an organisation established in 1985 with the aim of working with the rural poor.

Underemployment and poverty

There are over 250 million *khet majoor* (agricultural labourers) in India. Not only do they earn hardly enough to live on when in employment, but there are long periods when employment is scarce. The lean periods—between harvest and planting—can last up to six months, during which many labourers migrate to the towns in search of alternative employment.

The problems of underemployment, faced by both men and women, are particularly acute in the southern delta region of West Bengal. With high rainfall and good soils, allowing three crops a year, West Bengal has the highest rice production figures in India [1]. But it also carries a population of some 60 million people in an area of under 100,000 sq km. At 614 people per square kilometre, the population density is almost as high as in Bangladesh.

Poverty is widespread. Landless labourers account for 25% of the working population; if you include those who derive part of their income from labouring, the percentage rises to over 55%. They can expect to earn only about 20 rupees (61 US cents) a day. Seventy per cent of the farmers in the state have landholdings of under one hectare. Land is also very fragmented, with farmers having to work an average of seven separate small fields. With a high degree of sharecropping, this all discourages investment in the land.

Mechanisation has depleted the rural job market. Anil Tanti is from Raghabpur village, inhabited mainly by *adivasis* (tribal people), who are ruled over by *barnahindus* (high caste people). With four mouths to feed and only seven months' work a year at best, he finds it difficult to fend off hunger. "With the tractors the rich have brought in, there's even less work for us now," he says. He gets 20 rupees (61 US cents) a day doing agricultural work in the village, or 30 rupees (91 US cents) repairing roads in nearby Basirhat town, though he thinks that given the rate of inflation he should really get 32 rupees (97 US cents).

Landless labourers are lucky if they manage two meals a day. "We can't afford to eat the rice we grow," says Rukeya Begum of Ghoradol village. "It is sold in Calcutta market. Instead we buy *khud* [discarded rice grains] at 6 rupees [18 US cents] a kilo—you town people won't be able to eat it if I ask you to stay on for lunch. Cooking twice a day is a luxury, both for lack of fuel and rice."

Kabita Bera of Uttar Gayadham village, somehow ekes out a

living for herself and her daughter as her husband has left her—a common occurrence. "Many make do with snails and boiled rice day after day," she says, adding that the children often refuse to eat.

Deprivation of this kind has been denied by government ministers. Binny Chowdhury, West Bengal's minister of land and land reform, said in 1991 that although 15 years ago villagers did not get two meals a day, this kind of situation no longer existed [2]. However, statistics show that while nutritional status improved somewhat during the 1970s, there was some decline in daily calorie supply per capita during the 1980s [3].

The saline water of the delta area is ideal for prawn culture. Large corporations have arrived, bringing a big boom in pisciculture for export. Swapna Triparthy observes: "Though my family has been in prawn farming, we don't even know the taste of lobsters. We can't afford to. The best of the bananas in the backyard are kept for selling. We never get to eat them."

The increasing demand for vegetables in Calcutta and surrounding towns has seen many plots near ponds being turned into vegetable patches. Pond water is being used to irrigate these, and is also becoming contaminated owing to the use of fertilisers on the plots. Drinking water, already scarce because so much of the water in the delta area is brackish, is becoming even harder to find and some "owners" of ponds are selling water—turning a resource which used to be shared into an individual commercial asset.

Lack of drinking water, health services and sanitary facilities constitutes another major hazard for the rural population: diseases such as diarrhoea and gastroenteritis. The dangers are greatest in the rainy season. Frequent illnesses and death make fertile ground for superstition to flourish, which militates against practical action for progress.

The politicians' record

Since 1977, West Bengal has been ruled by a left-wing coalition called the Left Front, of which the Communist Party Marxist-Leninist (CPM) is the senior partner. It has implemented a land reform programme, which has seen the redistribution of approximately one million acres (405,000 hectares) of land to tribal people and scheduled castes (lowest castes which receive

In rural India, cycle-vans are often the only available means of transport to take people to distant health centres.

preferential support through certain social programmes). However, despite many calls for the Green Revolution to come to West Bengal, there is still serious underinvestment in agriculture in the state.

The administrative system operates through units of descending size: the state is divided into *thanas*, which are subdivided into Blocks. A Block encompasses several villages. The *panchayats*, or village councils, have been the principle vehicle for implementing the state government's social policies. In theory they are democratic, but in practice they are often under the control of various factions, which precludes effective decision-making.

The government now reserves 30% of seats in the *panchayats* for women. But villagers point out that most of the elected women are merely fronts for their powerful husbands, who are sometimes members of the *panchayat* themselves. Bela Adak, an SMS activist, says: "We looked forward to working with them—being women, they could relate to women's problems.

But we found them uninterested, perhaps because they hardly knew what to do, and they had been pushed reluctantly into the post."

The West Bengal government has a poor record of spending on rural development. A 1990 report showed that its Integrated Rural Development Programme (IRDP) had "failed to change the lifestyle of the poor in West Bengal due to lack of serious efforts and macro-level and micro-level planning [4]".

The federal government's Department of Programme Implementation carried out an evaluation of the progress achieved in implementing a centrally-funded 20-point programme for the poor: West Bengal was rated 17th out of 25 states. The report showed that the state failed miserably in sectors including small-scale industry, health, drinking water supply, family planning, welfare activities for scheduled castes and tribals, and housing for the poor [5].

Sundari, Gauri Haldar and others in Gopalnagar village, which is mainly inhabited by scheduled castes, have many complaints: "Our houses crumble down, the roofs have holes or are torn apart. But the *morals (panchayat* heads) don't bother to come and see to it." *Panchayats* are allocated money specifically for repairing houses. Paban Haldar, a village leader and a *panchayat* member, alleges that better-placed people on the *panchayat* committee get the loans for repairs.

"The people do feel neglected," says Sanat Kanwar who also lives in the village. "When thatched roofs are blown away by cyclones, those with partially damaged roofs get 30 rupees [91 US cents] as compensation, while the maximum compensation is 200 rupees [US$6]. *Babus* [government officers] blow that much per head on a lunch engagement in Calcutta."

Life expectancy and literacy have not improved. Female literacy remains at around 30%, while just over 50% of men are literate [6]. Life expectancy still hovers around 51 years [7]. The West Bengal government launched a Child Survival and Safe Motherhood scheme in 1992-93, with the target of reducing infant mortality to below 60 per 1,000 live births and the maternal mortality rate to under 200 per 100,000 live births by the year 2000 [8]. Many doubt that this is achievable.

A platform for the rural working class

With the aim of helping the rural poor, Jana Sanghati Kendra (JSK) (Centre for People's Solidarity) was formed in 1985 by social researchers Anuradha Talwar (now secretary of the organisation), Swapan Ganguli and a few of their colleagues. "We felt we should move to the villages, to the grassroots, if we really wanted to work for the deprived," says Talwar. "Sitting in Calcutta, we did some work but it was more seminars and workshops than in-depth work. We didn't know very well how the poorest of the poor lived—what needed to be done to improve their life. We felt the need to create a platform for the rural working class—the largest yet most unorganised and neglected section in India."

JSK's aim is to contribute towards changing unequal social structures and to encourage the deprived to claim their "right to live" in a democratic society. Its objectives are: to help agricultural labourers, marginal farmers, rural women and other disadvantaged people to come together in activity-based organisations; to work in solidarity with other similar organisations, through joint campaigns and struggles; to organise and develop community-based programmes; and to take short-term "project" measures to meet the immediate needs of the rural poor, which avoid undermining the long-term goal of building a strong, united mass organisation, based on democratic participation.

Jainal Abedin is from Purandarpur village. After graduation in 1982, he searched in vain for a job. He wanted a white collar job, as these are deemed to be more "respectful". In 1992, after a decade of frustration, he joined JSK. "I had a lot of dreams when I was a college boy. But as year after year I remained unemployed, my hopes subsided. When the JSK people came to our area with their ideas about improving our rural lot, their constructive approach, their assurance that we can do something if we are strong, I was inspired."

Ganguli says that they work in a genuinely democratic way. All the decisions are taken by people directly involved in the work. This is ensured by having open discussions at the regular meetings. "A member can even bring to our notice if another is seen spending beyond their means and the accused can be confronted, since it denotes corruption and we can't allow that. Not that discussions involving members always end satisfactorily. Sometimes there are acrimonious scenes. But the workers are now getting used to this new culture, or discipline, or whatever you call it."

Landless labourers join hands

As JSK's activities expanded, so it changed structurally. In 1988, it helped to found PBKMS as a mass organisation of the agricultural poor. It also found that women workers needed their own platform for their specific problems, so a separate organisation, Shramjeevi Mahila Samity (SMS) (Women Labourers' Organisation), was established in 1990. In the same year, a cultural wing, Jana Sanskriti, was formed, inviting participation from the middle classes who were rather weary of politics, and spreading the message of a need to change existing social evils.

A series of wage struggles in villages in the Mathurapur Block of South 24 Parganas led to the formation of PBKMS. The villagers realised that only a strong and broadly-based organisation could push through their demands. They contacted other like-minded groups, and in April 1988, a convention was organised for agricultural labourers in Calcutta. Attended by 1,400 workers, it was a tremendous success.

As a result, PBKMS was formed as an independent mass organisation of agricultural labourers, peasants and village artisans. Anil Tanti from Raghabpur village feels that "joining hands with other landless labourers has strengthened our position. Previously the *baralaks* [powerful elites] used to beat us up on the slightest pretext. They would cut the jute from other people's fields and pass the blame on to us. Now that we've banded together, they've stopped. They realise that the situation is different now."

Unlike most similar organisations, PBKMS is not affiliated to any political party. Individual members may support particular parties, but within PBKMS they are expected to work in a nonpartisan way. This can entail skilful tightrope-walking, particularly in West Bengal villages where the ruling CPM and the opposition Congress are sharply polarised.

"People got so used to party politics that they couldn't believe there could be any organisation without party affiliation," says veteran worker Nitai Pramanik of Raidighi Centre. "But when JSK started contacting the young people, discussing the problems faced by villagers, whether leftist or rightist, and projects to tackle them, slowly there was a response from the people."

Rabindranath Haldar of Gopalnagar village, who was once a teacher, joined PBKMS because of the failures of party politics. "Even from school days I dreamt of building a new society. I got involved in politics and did some social work. But I soon got disillusioned, when I saw the poor remaining where they were. At election time, politicians come and talk sympathetically about landless labourers, but after getting the votes, they forget. They get busy with promoting their own kith and kin, and we remain where we are."

Disillusionment with mainstream politics and politicians is a common complaint, well expressed in two songs used by PBKMS in their cultural activities, and beautifully sung by Chittaranjan Pramanik of Pathar Pratima:

Oh, what a fate!
They came before the election —
Promised us IRDP, roads.
Now where has he gone?
Don't give us dreams.
If we rely on him,
We'll lose whatever we have.
Our children will starve.

They speak of the country,
Their children go to school,
Their wives are like fair radishes.
Our women are dust of the road,
My stomach hides a fire of hunger.

Swapna Triparthy says that, at first, people were suspicious of PBKMS, but were won over by their actions. "The road you have just driven on was in a shambles. There was no public transport and people had difficulty going to the nearest town or Calcutta. We met the BDO [Block Development Officer—the local government administrator], even the deputy magistrate, and sent numerous deputations, but it was no use. So we decided on a road blockade. We didn't allow any vehicle to pass through. The administration had to give in and public transport to Calcutta was introduced. The villagers were very grateful. They came out spontaneously to support us. Even from villages where PBKMS was not active, people came and asked us to go there to help solve their local problems. Their opinion about us changed."

Although these kinds of action have led to PBKMS acquiring a revolutionary image in some quarters, on the whole politicians express their admiration. Narayan Mukherjee, Communist Party member for Basirhat, North 20 Parganas, says: "I've seen them fighting for a minimum wage. At a political level, we too are working for the same aim. I've seen them taking part in local cultural activities, arranging meetings at the local book fair to spread social messages. Good work indeed."

The Employment Guarantee Act

Demands for an Employment Guarantee Act (EGA) have existed in India since the early 1970s. The basis of this is that when unable to find work in agriculture, labourers should be employed by the government on capital works schemes or other employment programmes at a minimum wage. Employment has been guaranteed in this way in Maharashtra state (West) since 1979; the scheme is operative in some districts of Andhra Pradesh and is soon to be implemented in Tamil Nadu. After a campaign of national seminars, rallies and conventions, the short-lived Janata Dal government of V P Singh was on the verge of implementing the EGA when it fell from power. Even the cost of the EGA had been calculated: at 12,000 crore rupees (US$3.6 billion) per year for the entire country.

PBKMS is campaigning for the introduction of the EGA in West Bengal. It organised a relay hunger strike of 1,700

Swapna Triparthy, Tahamina Begum and Shaktipada Bar outside the PBKMS centre in Milonmore. The sign proclaims: "The right to work is our birthright".

agricultural labourers (40% of them women) in 1992. Street corner meetings are held every month, and the practice of *gherao* (surrounding somebody until a promise is extracted) has also been used. A motion was put forward in the 1994 winter session of the Legislative Assembly that the EGA be implemented: the state government agreed, but put the onus on central government.

PBKMS argues that an effective EGA can be introduced if ordinary people are allowed to participate at the planning stage and if the scheme is extended to the whole year rather than just the lean season. It believes that funding can be found by combining existing employment programmes, through income tax and by transferring the subsidy on amenities such as cooking gas, which largely benefit the middle classes.

Not everyone agrees that the EGA can successfully tackle rural poverty. One dissenter is Hut Gurudas Dasgupta, a CPM MP, who headed the Parliamentary Committee on Rural Labour. "I don't believe", he says, "on the basis of facts, that enaction of the EGA in some states of the country has been able to bring appreciable changes in the life and livelihood of farmers.... It can at best be a temporary unemployment benefit." Dasgupta, who is also vice-president of PB Rajya Khet Majoor Union, the agricultural labour wing of the CPM, makes a strong case for agricultural labourers to join trade unions so that they can enjoy the same benefits as industrial labourers: such things as health insurance, disability pensions and old-age pensions.

Organisations like PBKMS will continue to fight for the EGA. But it is always difficult to maintain a united front. "Even among landless labourers there are different political affiliations", says Rabindranath Haldar, "and arriving at a solution is often a problem. A common platform is needed to get recognition under the Indian constitution. Then the EGA movement will be successful."

Harekrishna Ghosh of Bansberia village supports the EGA but sounds a note of caution. "Somebody asked me: if the law is passed, shall we get the benefits? I said, not necessarily: we must fight for the implementation also."

The campaign for fair wages

One of the main demands of PBKMS concerns minimum wages. "We have fights—mostly verbal—with the *maliks* [landowners] for the right wages," says Indrani Sardar, a young *khet majoor*. The labour inspector employed by the government is supposed to come and report on whether we're getting the minimum stipulated wages, but he hardly ever comes." Agricultural labourers in Raghabpur allege that these inspectors are often hand-in-glove with the *maliks*. But recently, following a stream of complaints, they have been compelled to visit villages. Sukumar Gain says that before being told by PBKMS, many *khet majoor* did not even know of the existence of such officials.

Constant pressure by PBKMS has resulted in establishing minimum wage levels in some villages in South 24 Parganas. But this has created other problems. Nitai Guriya, a former *panchayat* member, points out that many middle class people who used to employ *khet majoor* now think better of paying the higher wage and work in the fields themselves. Anuradha Talwar, while admitting that this happens in a few places, insists that the majority of *khet majoor* have benefited.

Women still receive less pay, a difference of almost eight rupees a day (24 US cents) in Raghabpur village. In North 24 Parganas, where women work in the fields, this discrimination is widespread. SMS activists like Kalpana Sardar tell them to demand the same wage. "But they say: 'Can a woman be like a man?'" Nonetheless, SMS continues to campaign for equal pay and in some places has been successful.

Sukumoni Tanti, a tribal woman from Raghabpur village, works as a labourer in the fields whenever she can find work. She is paid around 15 rupees (45 US cents) a day, whereas men receive 22 rupees (67 US cents). Asked whether she complains, she says: "Oh, even if we do, they don't listen. 'How can a woman be equal to a man?' they say." Gauri Sardar, of the same village, says she is paid 12 rupees (36 US cents), while her husband gets 20 rupees (61 US cents). Clearly, wage payments are pretty arbitrary. "We women should do it together," says Gauri. "What's the point of my shouting alone?—it's only a drop in the ocean. Not all of them join me. Perhaps they are afraid that whatever work they have will be lost."

Combating violence against women

In a conservative social milieu, where women are given second class status, it is encouraging that SMS is so active. There are a number of issues, such as the need for tubewells, that women feel very strongly about.

SMS has taken a very active role, side by side with PBKMS, in demolishing illegal liquor dens and gambling joints. According to Swapna Triparthy, the strong presence of women in these campaigns reflects the relationship between heavy drinking by men and the increase in violence against women.

"I've noticed in my own village people have started drinking heavily, which was not there before. Gambling and, of late, mushrooming video halls showing mostly Hindi films from Bombay, with a surfeit of violence, rape and vulgar dances have only added to women's problems," she says. She expresses regret that the slow disappearance of *kirtan, jatra* and *jalsa*, traditional dances with a religious and moral message, seem to have eroded societal values. She says that men's drinking also puts a heavy financial burden on women as their husbands often use the money meant for household expenses.

The direct action taken by SMS and PBKMS has created great tension in some areas, especially since there are powerful vested interests in these liquor joints. Women have sometimes been threatened with physical assault for their participation in the campaign.

A large part of the work of SMS revolves around *salishi*, an indigenous method of imparting justice through intervention and counselling, without going to the courts. Most of the complaints come from wives facing ill-treatment from husbands or in-laws. A *salishi* we attended at the Milonmore Centre was held to intervene in a case between an estranged couple. The woman had run away to the PBKMS centre from her husband's home because she could no longer bear the continual harassment by her in-laws. Representatives of the local village *panchayat*, the husband and members of SMS were present. The arguments presented throw some light on the power relations between men and women in West Bengal homes.

The husband complained that his wife did not help at home and was a reluctant wife in other ways too. He was, however, unable to explain why he kicked her in the stomach when she was nine months pregnant, leading to a still-born baby. The wife, on the other hand, alleged that she had proof that he was having an affair with his older brother's wife under the same roof. After prolonged discussions, the *salishi* ruled that the wife should be given a plot of land by her husband and that she should no longer be harassed. Thus a divorce was avoided—a terrible stigma for a woman, who always ends up the loser.

The reputation that SMS justice is impartial and sympathetic appears to have spread among women. That women feel able to step outside the home and air their grievances—especially in

A married couple leaving a *salishi* after it has ruled in the wife's favour.

conservative South 24 Parganas, where women do not usually work in the fields—represents a significant advance. Now even Muslim women come to SMS, sometimes surreptitiously, to request intervention on their behalf.

SMS activists like Swapna Triparthy are also very conversant with legal intricacies and know how to take on the system. Recently, they succeeded in getting an assistant sub-inspector of police from the Pathar Pratima Block transferred elsewhere, because he refused to act on the basis of a first information report (FIR) from a rape victim: if a case is made "FIR" it means that the suspect can be arrested immediately. In this particular case, the rape victim was compelled by powerful members of the community to retract her statement. Because of SMS pressure, it has also been made mandatory that any report of a criminal offence against a woman, not just rape, should be given the status of an FIR.

SMS activists regularly stage plays, conceived by Jana Sanskriti members, with social messages against violence and other problems commonly faced by women. Villagers are used to folk entertainment and the plays gradually have an effect. Moreover, the Forum Theatre, as the group run by SMS is called, helps the women participants to change roles, playing the parts of oppressor and oppressed, and exploring solutions to their problems.

The demand for tubewells

An evaluation by the Union (federal) government in 1991 of a scheme to supply villages with drinking water showed that West Bengal completed work in only 982 villages out of a targeted 2,053 [9]. The steady decline of traditional water sources and the high incidence of disease caused by the drinking of contaminated water have led to a great demand for tubewells, which each cost around 40,000 rupees (US$1,200). The existing number is pitifully small. In Raghabpur village, for example, there is only one tubewell for 1,500 people. Gauri Haldar, an SMS activist, says that if the tubewell breaks down, they have to walk for more than a kilometre to fetch water.

"Cholera is widespread in our village," says Anil Tanti. "Tubewell water is kept stored for a long time since women living far away from a tubewell find it difficult to collect water every day. We need at least five or six tubewells in the village. When we go with petitions to the BDO, the *pradhan* [village leader] or *panchayat* members, they assure us that one day we'll get them. But nothing happens."

Where there is no tubewell, fetching water from neighbouring villages can be difficult. Ashara Maity, a housewife in Enathpur village explains: "We are 250-300 households and we don't have a tubewell. If children are sent to fetch water from the next village where there is one, the people there scold them or they have to stand in long queues."

"A few days ago", Ashara continues, "I was busy in the kitchen, so I sent my young daughter to collect the water. She came back with a head injury. She had slipped on the wet ground. There's only one pond in the village, belonging to a *malik*. If we go there to wash utensils or anything, he abuses us. Now, our main concern is how to get approval for a tubewell. Or how can we get a loan to dig a pond?" She says that a

When a village has no tubewell, people from neighbouring villages are not always willing for theirs to be used.

petition by women has been presented to the local *panchayat* committee.

The allocation of a tubewell is usually decided by the Block Development Office and the *panchayat*. But villagers point out that favouritism often dictates these decisions. The worst sufferers are women. A major task for the activists of SMS is mobilising women and men to rally together to demand tubewells. They write petitions, collect signatures and place them before officials.

The practice of *gherao* is also used. "In Digambarpur-Raipur we had been appealing for a tubewell, writing petitions a number of times but they said there was no quota," says Alpana Das, who was once a housemaid, taught herself to read and write, and became an activist. "Fed up, we *gheraoed* the officials with women carrying empty vessels. They had to give in, and within two weeks they had arranged it."

Health campaigns and alternative medicine

The same evaluation report shows that the performance of the Health Department has been lamentable. Between 1990 and 1991, the West Bengal government did not set up a single health sub-centre, although it had a target of 796. Only 15 of the planned 33 primary health centres were established. Only five of the planned 19 community health centres were commissioned. The West Bengal government's target is one sub-centre for every 5,000 inhabitants in the plains, and one for every 3,000 in the hilly areas. In reality, a sub-centre serves 10,000 to 12,000 people [10].

Most villages have no proper health centre. And those health centres that do exist lack medicines; 80 of the 120 medicines listed by the Health Department have been dropped because of a lack of funds. An order issued in October 1991 reduced the

A typically delapidated government health centre at Bhadia in North 24 Parganas.

number of drugs to 30 for inpatients and 18 for outpatients. "They have the same old tablet for all ailments. We don't have faith in their curing power so we've stopped going there," says a woman in Raghabpur. In North 24 Parganas, the Ghola subsidiary hospital has an abandoned look. "The doctor doesn't come every day. Even if he does, he stays only for two or three hours. Most of the medicines are not available. He brings some, but takes them with him when he goes back," say Rashid and Ahmad Gazi, two Muslim youths from neighbouring Sadarpur village.

"Stomach problems haunt us throughout the year," says Gauri Sardar. "Many of the old medicines our forefathers knew are lost to us, but we are benefiting from the homeopathic medicines given at the [PBKMS] centre. But with cases of snake bite or suicide attempts [through the common practice of swallowing poison], patients have to be taken on cycle-vans to the nearest health centre 15 km away. As for latrines, we're poor people. The government should provide them."

Another villager, Mohammed Sheikh of Digambarpur, says: "Before I describe my ailment, the doctor asks me to go to a particular shop where he himself sells the medicines allotted for the villagers." He also points out that although these centres are located in some of the most snake-infested areas, there is no anti-venom serum. Deaths from snake bite in the summer and during the monsoon are common, and people often resort to going to the *ujha* (traditional doctor) in the hope of a cure. "All they have is a bit of Dettol, cotton wool and a few tablets", says one Haripur villager. Many villagers also allege that even seriously ill patients are not treated properly if they do not belong to the political party the doctor prefers.

In 1991, out of a budget of 459 crore rupees (US$139 million), only 66 crore rupees (US$20 million) was spent on medicine, food for patients, treatment and accessories, while the rest was spent on staff salaries [11]. Most government doctors refuse to do the three-year rural posting stipulated in their training agreement.

PBKMS activists try to tackle this problem in two ways: by forcing health officials to function properly, and by providing alternative treatment. Alpana Das cites the example of a doctor at

Mathurapur hospital. "He took 10 rupees (30 US cents) per patient, though he was not supposed to. We also had evidence that he sold medicine outside. We organised a petition and got about 600 signatures and confronted the doctor. He admitted his guilt and promised not to charge fees for treatment."

PBKMS centres now have trained homeopaths who treat villagers. Naresh Ghosh of Raghabpur village is a young man with a family of four. Unemployed and frustrated, he came across PBKMS, liked their ideas and joined them. He was trained at Badu in homeopathic treatment and now works among the poor tribal villagers of Raghabpur, treating about 15 patients a day.

As medicines are expensive and the poor cannot afford them, JSK is trying to revive old health cures, according to Anuradha Talwar. There are 36 dispensaries run in different villages. Training and orientation courses are regularly organised at the Badu centre.

Arjun Das is active in the local PBKMS branch in Haripur village, which runs a homeopathic clinic. This is a poor village, and even the tiny sum of two rupees for annual club membership is left unpaid by many members. There is only one tubewell for this and two adjacent villages. "Health care is almost nil," he says. "So people flock to our clinic."

Ashara Maity organised an SMS meeting in her village at which 10 out of 30 mothers reported that their children suffered from stomach problems. She made a list of the children and organised transport to take them to the PBKMS clinic in a neighbouring village. When she arrived she found there were 70 mothers wanting their children to go.

Many women complain about the lack of sanitation. All bar the well-to-do have to go to the open fields. During the monsoon, they make do near inhabited areas, even near ponds, as they cannot go far along muddy roads. "The government has practically no programme for sanitation," says Anuradha Talwar. UNICEF, jointly with Lokshiksha Parishad of Ramakrishna Mission, runs a sanitation programme in Midnapore District. This is a self-funding scheme, where villagers are charged on a sliding scale from 230 to 2,070 rupees (US$7-63) per sanitary pit.

According to UNICEF officials in Calcutta, the programme has been very successful, but few people in other villages seem to have heard of it. When asked if she would invest 230 rupees in a sanitary pit, Sundari, an SMS member from Anandapur, says: "Where would I get the money? When I can't manage to eat, how can I afford to think of it?"

No time for learning

Tapas Sardar belongs to a scheduled caste in Bansberia-Jaffarpur and is top of his class at Ballavpur High School, a 5-km walk from home. Buying books is a great problem: his father is a landless labourer, who has regular work for only three months of the year and otherwise tries to make ends meet by selling things like home-made brooms, or doing odd jobs. "Every year we think will be his last in school", says Tapas' mother, "but until now, with God's grace and help from his kind teacher and his sister Ashta, who collect books from old students, we have managed."

Tuni dries her *gamcha*. She will wrap herself in this when she needs to wash her only set of clothes.

Many girls are not so lucky. On the way to Milonmore, we stop on the road to speak to two young girls. Tuni is drying her *gamcha*, taking advantage of the breeze, while her friend keeps watch over two grazing goats. Asked if they go to school, Tuni replies: "No, where's the time? There's so much work at home. Besides, we have to look after the goats."

When so many have received little or no education as children, there is a great need for adult education. In 1991, the West Bengal government won an award from UNESCO in recognition of the "spectacular" success of its Total Literacy Programme. However, there are widespread claims that figures have been inflated and that lack of follow-up means many people lapse back into illiteracy [12]. Anandamohan Haldar of Jagadishpur village, who was himself on the *panchayat* committee for five years, says that literacy is "on paper only".

Draupadi Sardar from the tribal-dominated village of Raghabpur is very proud that she can sign her name now, thanks to SMS training. "I was illiterate. They've helped me to realise my dream," she says. But other women say they cannot make SMS classes. Chitra Haldar, from Jaffarpur village, explains: "We've so much work at home, we have little time for the weekly meeting. We're poor. Work comes first.... Things like literacy will have to come later."

Bela Adak says that literacy and numeracy are the first steps but that "social education is more important—to realise where we are financially, politically, culturally. Just bookish knowledge is not enough."

Credit and income generation

PBKMS runs savings and loan schemes. Individuals put a little money every month into a common fund kept in a post office savings account. They can borrow when in need, without paying interest, and repay slowly. Bela Adak says that this has saved people from the clutches of the moneylenders and instilled self-confidence.

PBKMS and SMS activists make it clear that they cannot offer finance; they can only help people secure their rights and improve their lot. Under SMS guidance, women in the Pathar

Pratima Block enthusiastically took part in the government's nursery garden development programme and later sold the saplings they grew at a profit. With her share of the profit, Malati Manna bought a cycle-van for her husband. Kabita Bera bought a plot of land, and Renuka bought back a piece of land her father had had to sell off.

Swapna Triparthy says pragmatically: "We got the saplings free from the government, but when we gave them for planting to the SMS workers, we charged a small sum [10 paise—under one US cent] per tree. People always take care of things more if they have to pay for it, even a little sum."

In the southern villages of 24 Parganas, women do not work in the fields as they do further north, in the tribal areas. They have, therefore, a greater capacity to take on income-generating activities. Altarani Sardar, of Jaffarpur village, for example, augments her *khet majoor* husband's income by doing odd jobs in rich people's homes and by making *datans* (traditional toothbrushes). "I don't get money every day. Sometimes monthly, sometimes every other month. There's no security."

Changing the mould

Clearly, progress is variable. Insecurity of employment anddaily struggle for survival explain why people cannot avail themselves of the educational opportunities that exist. Campaigning for guaranteed employment and fair wages therefore remain overriding concerns, and so far success in these areas has been elusive.

JSK and its sister organisations attribute what success they have had in West Bengal villages to their democratic and participatory way of working. Anuradha Talwar believes this also ensures continuation of the work, adding that most NGOs are centralised, and dominated by charismatic individuals: "If they withdraw from an area the work stops." Naresh Ghosh, from Raghabpur, is optimistic that the work started by SMS will continue, even if they withdraw from the area, especially since "the women are very strong here—even stronger than the men on social issues".

"The development we talk about involves the rights and

responsibilities of people," says Swapan Ganguli. "We put great emphasis on developing human character and values. Only then can they also keep tabs on their elected representatives. We don't want political power, but those elected must be answerable to the needs of the people they represent; we want to reset the society. Current societal values are not acceptable to us. We don't expect radical change: the mould has to be changed. Our aim is to make people conscious of their aims and demand those benefits that can mean real development for them."

In Defence of Women

Fighting for equal rights in Uganda

Traditionally regarded as part of their husbands' property, and severely disadvantaged under customary law, Ugandan women are beginning to claim their legal rights to property, custody of children, and protection from marital violence. The Ugandan branch of the International Federation of Women Lawyers (FIDA) is helping women gain protection under the law, campaigning for an end to discriminatory laws, and taking legal education into the villages—where it is hampered by male opposition. **Sarah Mirembe** talks to FIDA staff and beneficiaries and looks at non-participatory service provision. Photographs by **Laura Mulenga**.

Inside a yellow-painted building, about 40 women are waiting, some looking excited, others dejected. There is silence. Some are sitting on benches but others prefer to queue, even if it means standing for as long as three hours, braving tiredness and hunger.

These women are not lining up for treatment in a government hospital, nor waiting to vote candidates on to Resistance Councils (RCs), Uganda's village authorities. They are clients of FIDA, an organisation of women lawyers which gives free legal assistance to underprivileged people. The building is FIDA's headquarters and legal aid clinic, attended by women from in and around Kampala.

Twice as poor as before

In the decades following independence, Uganda has suffered greatly. Years of civil war and political unrest resulted in the almost complete disintegration of the social and economic fabric of the nation.

Uganda's GNP per capita stood at US$250 in 1989, having shrunk at an average of 2.8% per year between 1965 and 1989 [1], the worst record of any low-income country. This means that Uganda's people are, on average, twice as poor (or half as well-off) as they they were in 1965. For years, the steadily declining price of coffee, Uganda's principal export crop, had a drastic impact. It is only very recently that a surge in world coffee prices has started to benefit the Ugandan economy.

The country is deeply in debt: its debt service costs as a percentage of exports shot up from 13% in 1980 to 77% in 1989 [2]. The resulting structural adjustment programme is forcing the Ugandan government to slash drastically its social programme in education and health.

Between 1960 and 1992, life expectancy dropped from 43 to 42.6 years, while developing countries as a whole saw a rise from 46.2 to 63 years during the same period. The proportion of the population with access to clean drinking water fell from 35% in 1975 to 15% in 1991, while other developing countries doubled their share from 36% to 70%. Infant mortality fell only slightly: from 133 per 1,000 live births in 1960 to 104 in 1992 (compared to 30 in Europe and 69 in the developing world) [3]. The adult literacy rate grew much more slowly than the average, as did school enrolments.

The rural population has suffered disproportionately. Urban people are four times more likely than rural people to have access to clean drinking water and twice as likely to have access to sanitation. There are 13.2 million rural people living in absolute poverty—75% of the population [4].

Government services have been in decline. In Ntengeru, Mukono District, for example, the roads are now deeply potholed, almost turning into footpaths. One woman, who declines to be named, says that the road used to be wide enough for two trucks to pass through. "In the past, [it] used to be graded at least once a year, but now no more. We tried using our hands and hoes to make the road, but it was useless. We lost interest because the government was not helping us," she says. As in many of the villages we visited, there are clear signs of malnutrition among children.

Government support to education has also been cut to the bone: only 10% of the costs of primary education are now met by the state [5]. Ssalongo, a civil servant recently made redundant, charts the decline in educational opportunities: "In the old days, you would be sure of having your child educated from Senior One to university free of charge. But that has changed." Now high schools charge fees and "these days, we hear that the government is introducing fees at Makerere University. We are just at the end of the road," he says. "Now, I cannot even pay school fees for my little children to go to primary school. But even if I educated them, where are the jobs when they are chasing us from work? In those days, whoever went to university was sure of getting a job and a car. These days, it is only the rich who get good jobs because they can pay bribes or they have rich godfathers who can influence the employer."

In the 1970s and early 1980s, Uganda's human rights record hit rock bottom. Hundreds of thousands were killed. Freedom of expression was non-existent. Under President Museveni's rule, things have been getting better, although there is still a significant lack of freedom of expression for political parties and, to some degree, the press.

The burden on women

Women suffered particularly badly during those tragic decades. The number of female-headed households increased to as much as 70% in some districts. Many women have been widowed as a result of war or AIDS, and many have been divorced or abandoned by their husbands.

Even without these tragedies, women are extremely disadvantaged. They receive only a third of the years of schooling of their male counterparts, and half as many women as men are literate.

Rural women are usually very isolated as communications are very poor. In 1989, only 43% of households had radio sets or could listen to their neighbour's set [6]. And even if a family has a radio, the cost of batteries is very high, a severe restriction on use. Listening to the radio has, anyway, long been a man's privilege, and women have little opportunity to choose programmes. "I never think about listening to [the] radio because my parents taught me that it is only men who listen to radio, just like eating chicken and eggs," says Nambozo Masaba, a woman from the rural area of Mbale.

Ugandan women are responsible for 80% of Uganda's food, providing about 70% of the total agricultural labour [7]. They are principally but not exclusively confined to the unpaid subsistence sector, and carry out their agricultural tasks without the benefit of technological innovation, inputs or finance [8]. Women have primary responsibility for household management, childrearing, food preparation, care of the sick and the elderly, and family health and welfare. Although they work on average 15 hours a day, their work is not fully recognised in official statistics or by policymakers because it is mostly done at home—where it is unremunerated—or outside the formal economy.

Women, law and custom

There are few national laws which are blatantly discriminatory, says Winnie Sekadde, FIDA's treasurer. It is more in their application, where cultural norms play a important role, that women suffer. "A poor woman", says Sekadde, "will be dependent at all levels, which will affect her bargaining power." Equally, a poor woman who has been mistreated is unable to afford a lawyer's services.

In rural areas in particular, where all government services are at a very low level, women expect and receive little support from the law. For example, notes Sekadde, if a deserted mother sues for maintenance, the court will order the father to pay 2,000 Ugandan shillings (US$2.15) a month, which will sustain a child for little more than a day. The mother bears the responsibility for providing for the child for the rest of the month.

"Customary laws are...antagonistic to the woman," says

Women provide 70% of total agricultural labour in Uganda, but they have no legal right to own land.

Sekadde. "She is expected to sit silently while proceedings go on, and if she wants to raise a point, she has to do so through somebody else, usually a man, which carries its own disadvantages." In such a setting, women have very little chance to appeal. Whatever the decision, they are expected to accept it as binding and final, and any questioning of it is seen as contempt for the elders or clan leaders.

Ugandan rural society is dominated by other cultural norms that discriminate heavily against women. In most Ugandan cultures, a woman is not allowed to own or inherit land or property. At marriage, she is bought like an asset in exchange for a substantial bride price and is then entirely dependent on her husband. Many girls are married off at a tender age—15 or even younger—to men they barely know. Especially in rural areas, it is common for a widow to be obliged to marry a relative of her late husband.

Women's rights have become an issue only quite recently, Sekadde points out. For the first 20 years of independence, the most basic human rights were being violated, even the right to life. In that climate, there was little room for the advancement of women. But during the last seven years or so, during which the country has achieved some semblance of peace, it has been recognised that women's rights have all along been violated. Lobby groups for human rights, and women's rights in particular, have sprung up, and women's voices are now being heard.

"What has changed", says Sekadde, "is that hitherto ignorant women have now been made aware that they have rights and that there are different avenues to obtain redress when their rights are violated. Women are no longer sitting in the background to take whatever comes, but are also speaking out to get help and to help their fellow women."

The government has promoted women's rights by creating a Ministry for Women in Development, with active campaigns to eliminate discriminatory laws on marriage, divorce, and education, amongst other things. These campaigns are being waged particularly within the context of a constitutional review, and 43 women were recently elected to the Constituent Assembly, which is to write the new constitution.

Gradually, more women are becoming involved in politics and business, competing with men in almost every field in a bid to strengthen their social and economic standing. Parliament has women members, and there are women heads of department. But it is mostly urban educated women who are taking these prominent roles, and who are aware of their rights. Rural society is still governed by customary laws.

On the economic level, some progress is being made. An increasing number of women's organisations in rural areas are supporting income-generating activities, such as handicrafts, bricklaying and farming, which help empower women economically and reduce their dependence on their husbands.

FIDA and women's rights

FIDA Uganda is an affiliate of the Federación Internacional de Abogadas (International Federation of Women Lawyers), whose headquarters are in Spain. A group of women lawyers decided in 1974 to form FIDA Uganda after realising that most of their sisters were unaware of the law and of their rights. However, the organisation was able to become effective only in the late 1980s with the relative stability brought by the government of President Museveni's National Resistance Movement (NRM).

FIDA's major objective is twofold: to create awareness among rural people, especially the poor, of their rights and obligations; and second, to help women and children obtain effective protection under the law. FIDA is committed to encouraging stability within families through legal advice and counselling.

Today, the organisation also works as an active pressure group for law reform. Together with other women's organisations, it has been seeking to ensure that the new constitution embodies laws which offer equal opportunities and stimulate economic development for women as well as men. It believes that it is axiomatic that women should have the right to be as fully involved as men in all aspects of public life, and to be treated equally. FIDA has also identified laws, cultural practices and customs where women's dignity, welfare and interests are flouted, and has sought their prohibition under the new constitution.

Several of FIDA's proposals have been adopted in the draft constitution. It is up to women to ensure that the laws which discriminate against them are finally abolished, says Mary Maitum, the coordinator of the Women and the Constitution project within the Ministry for Women in Development. "It is for us women to rise up and defend our rights," she declares. "We must tell the Constituent Assembly delegates that we are also human beings. Rural women do not know where to go whenever their rights are abused. Sometimes they go to RCs, who are men...and are themselves often interested in grabbing their brothers' property and in abusing women."

Professor Tumwine Mukubwa, Dean of the Faculty of Law at Makerere University, a man and a strong supporter of women, agrees. "It is up to women to mobilise their fellow women in order to have the laws changed. We are not going to fight this war for you, you must do it and raise the consciousness of the men as well."

Taking the law to the people

Since 1986, FIDA has had a programme to raise awareness in people, especially women—about the law and their legal rights. It attempts to reach rural people by translating laws into local languages and by using radio. It has also started holding mobile

Making a point at a legal clinic in Kiyindi village.

legal clinics and education seminars in rural areas. Every weekend, FIDA members visit different rural areas to give both legal education and assistance to the poor. This work has been concentrated to date in Mukono, Mpigi, Kapchorwa, Mubende, Lira and Gulu Districts.

The major topics covered at the seminars are: how to understand and write wills (especially important with regard to land disputes and succession); the need to legalise marriages (important for the protection of women and their property if the husband deserts, divorces or dies); property rights; and defilement and rape. AIDS is also discussed. Underlying these themes is an active encouragement to women to believe in themselves and participate in economic activities.

The seminars involve both men and women because, according to Winnie Sekadde, it makes no sense to teach only women when the laws affect both sexes. While FIDA's original intention was to work with the poorest women and children, an inability to identify these groups has led to the door being opened to everyone, although the focus on women is maintained.

Response to the mobile legal education seminars has so far been poor. In July 1994, seminars in Mukono District had an average attendance of about 30 people. In at least three areas, no one turned up. All the people questioned said either that they were unaware of the seminar or that they had heard about it too late. Clearly, the local leaders are failing to mobilise the people in these areas, due in part to the fact that they are not paid for their work. Winnie Kibuuka, Secretary for Women in Ntengeru sub-county, Mukono District, says one problem is that "the information first gets to the RC chiefs, who are men. They are not bothered about things that touch women and will not bother to mobilise women to attend the seminar."

Another explanation may be that FIDA has not involved its target group in any participatory way. Instead of inviting rural people to express their views and aspirations, about the kind of assistance they want, the lawyers who make up FIDA's membership have themselves set the priorities. This may have had the effect of distancing, if not alienating, rural women, who are not able to identify directly with FIDA.

Lawyer Rebecca Kadaga is quick to defend FIDA: "Because FIDA is a professional organisation for only lawyers, there is no way we could bring in our target group, although our services are for the poorest of the poor."

Some men stop their wives attending meetings because they think they are just going to gossip, or learn "taboos" about their rights, which they believe will be bad for their marriages. Rebecca Kadaga says: "Some men blame FIDA for women becoming aggressive and learning about their rights, because enlightened women don't want to remain in the background any more." Women, too, sometimes still endorse this kind of thinking.

Jane, a FIDA member, says that "FIDA has acquired a bad name in some circles, especially among some men who think [it] is out to destroy their marriages—especially those whose cases are brought to us, because we have to call them and talk to them. Some men think that FIDA is infringing their natural rights to run the affairs of their family. Whenever we talk to some of these men, they always quarrel and castigate FIDA and all the women's rights activists. They would even like to ban the whole organisation if only they had the power." But Jane remains positive: "Where we have reached, there is no turning back. Those men have to accept this whether they want to or not," she says.

Elly Karuhanga, Constituent Assembly member for Nyabushozi, says he was fully converted to the cause of women's rights after FIDA member and activist Miriam Matembe explained to him what they were doing. "Men's poor opinions towards some of the women's organisations [arise] because the women never bother to educate the men as well. They lack the right approach to their issues," he says.

Professor Mukubwa claims that what some women activists demand is not what the majority of women in rural areas want. "Talking of equal representation on Boards of Directors, and three months' maternity leave is not very realistic. A village woman cannot even think of a thing like maternity leave." He says that most educated women live in urban areas and tend to "forget" that the majority of rural women who never went to school are not even aware of their basic rights.

High demand, few resources

Two clinics, in Kampala and Mbale, provide the main channel through which FIDA gives legal assistance to women. A high proportion of the cases it deals with concern divorce, land disputes, custody, maintenance and sexual offences.

Project worker Joseph Omuron acknowledges that in districts where FIDA does not operate "few people have any knowledge of the association and what opportunities it could offer them". Even the few poor women who are aware find it very difficult to travel to Kampala or Mbale for assistance because of transport costs—if, indeed, transport is available at all. Rebecca Kadaga says that it is within Kampala, Arua, Mbale and their suburbs that the organisation's impact can truly be felt.

FIDA is seriously understaffed. The Kampala clinic has only three full-time qualified lawyers to meet with all clients, while Mbale has one, with three part-time volunteers. FIDA's entire staff is only 24.

At the same time, the caseload is expanding rapidly. At the Kampala clinic it rose from 188 in 1988 to 2,198 in 1993. The Mbale clinic handled 221 cases in the first six months of 1994, as against a total caseload for all previous years of 422. FIDA project worker Joseph Omuron is candid about the difficulties: "We are overwhelmed by the number of clients, who range between 50 and 100 daily. We just do not have the capacity to assist all these clients."

As with most indigenous organisations, funding poses major problems. "Most of our funds come from foreign donors who often dictate what activities the money is to be spent on, although they may not be FIDA's priorities," Omuron says. A shortage of funds means that some of the proposed programmes have not been implemented.

Women and property rights

Talia Nansamba, 50, of Mukono District, was effectively abandoned by her husband after seven years of marriage. He left a local male leader in charge of the administration of his estate. "[This man] took over all the property, and sent me off the land which my husband had left for me," explains Talia. "He told me never to dare set foot on the land or even harvest anything. I had a plantation full of food. My late co-wife's daughter was also chased off.... We were helpless and desperate as we had nowhere to go. It was useless seeking help from the local authorities because they only listened to our despot."

Finally Talia went to FIDA for assistance. After a long struggle, the organisation succeeded in winning back the land on behalf of the Nansamba family.

Making a will is a crucial way in which women can protect property rights. Winnie Sekadde argues that "once a mother knows that she can make a will, then it is in her power to make her daughters financially independent by bestowing on them part of the property that she has earned". Women's response has been enthusiastic, but cultural norms are still based on the principle that women own nothing—even themselves—as everything is the property of the husband.

The current laws entitle widows to only 15% of their deceased husband's property, regardless of who has worked to acquire it. If it is the woman who dies, however, the widower automatically assumes ownership of all the property. Children are entitled to 75% of the inheritance, but it is always the boys who get the lion's share. FIDA believes that a woman should have the right to an adequate share of the property of their deceased husband, just as daughters should share equally with sons in the property of deceased parents. This would save many women from property disputes with opportunistic and greedy in-laws.

According to Solome Bossa, president of the Uganda Law Society (ULS), the majority of cohabiting couples in Uganda, although generally considered by society to be husband and wife, are not legally married. "I find it very painful", she laments, "to tell a woman who has been staying with her 'husband' for over 10 years that since you are not legally married, you have no right over the property."

Uganda's law recognises four types of marriage: those contracted in the church; customary marriages; marriages held in the District Executive Secretary's office; and marriages under Sharia law for Muslims. Marriage is often avoided because of the huge cost of the bride price. Moreover, many marriages in Uganda are polygamous. Except for Muslim marriages (Sharia allows a man to marry up to four wives), these unions are not legal and therefore not binding. The lack of binding contracts weakens women's legal position severely, and women's rights activists and ULS are campaigning for reform of the marriage laws. During a workshop organised by ULS in July 1994, it was recommended that a couple cohabiting for at least three years should gain legal status automatically.

Even if a woman is legally married, Ugandan law requires that for her to be able to claim property rights at the time of divorce, or when her husband dies, she must produce receipts as proof of purchase of the land.

Mary Mutonyi talks with a client at a FIDA clinic in Mbale.

Alice Nyegenye from Busua, who had been married for 20 years, lost her husband in a motor accident. He had not made a will, and his relatives immediately started grabbing his property. "We were traditionally married", says Alice, "although my husband had some other extra-marital affairs. We had acquired a lot of property but now they want to take everything from me." The relatives even tried to chase her out of the house, which she had bought together with her husband.

"Unfortunately", observes Mary Mutonyi, a voluntary lawyer working at FIDA's Mbale clinic, "no rural poor women keep receipts because it's the husbands who do the buying, whether it is the wife who worked for the money or not."

On three occasions, Alice's relatives were asked to come to the FIDA office for peace talks but each time they refused to attend. Finally, a team of FIDA members decided to visit their home in the presence of some local leaders. The visit helped Alice to regain some of her property.

Miriam Matembe suggests that the law should be changed to allow couples to share property equally at the time of divorce, as long as they have lived together for at least three years. In

September 1994, the Constituent Assembly rejected this proposal, for a number of reasons. It was argued that in many cultures in Uganda dowry is paid, so a woman has no reason to share the property. It was also argued that since the Christian church forbids divorce it would be wrong to pass a law that might encourage it. A further point made by opponents was that a law of this kind would cater only for privileged women because in rural areas there was almost no property to share.

Not daring to protest

Jovia lives in Nakifuma, Mukono District. She used to own a small shop with her husband, selling items such as soap, salt and sugar. Her husband was caught in the act of committing adultery and fined 600,000 shillings (US$645). To pay this, he sold off most of the property they had bought with their small business savings. She did not dare protest as she was aware that everything belonged to him.

"All my sweat and work has been used to pay for the folly of an encroaching woman," she says. "My husband is fond of selling my produce to go and feed other women. I used to complain at first until he threatened to chase me away. Both my father and mother-in-law warned me and told me to keep quiet if I wanted my marriage. So I just gave up and I try not to mind any more."

Jovia has three children in school, but she says her husband has abdicated all responsibility for them. "He neither pays school fees nor caters for their well-being," she says. "I have been doing everything from my small business earnings which he has now taken from me. Everything seems to be getting worse. These days he comes home only occasionally, mostly during the harvest time to sell our harvest. He keeps the money either for his girlfriends or drink. I am only lucky that he doesn't beat me as most husbands do in their homes."

Like Jovia, Eseza Kalinaki, also in Mukono, owned a shop that failed, thanks to her husband, Daniel. "I used to have a small hardware shop which had started to attract many customers. But when Daniel saw me making money, he decided to frustrate me. He took away all the money I had made, and all the facilities. And whenever he found a customer bargaining over a price, he would go home and beat me, claiming that I loved those men." Daniel closed the shop, and now Eseza sits at home.

"He does nothing but drink"

FIDA once wrote, about the experience of the average Ugandan woman: "From the moment she takes her first steps, she will be regarded as inherently inferior to her brother. She will continually be battling against prejudicial attitudes and unfair work practices in a culture that places little or no value on her contribution to society.... More often than not, she is regarded more as a productive piece of property than as a person—toiling long hours only for her husband to be paid."

Zahara, 48, a mother of eight and the second of three wives, says that she works "in the garden, the kitchen and the bedroom". The daily routine varies little. "I wake up at cockcrow daily, prepare breakfast for my husband and children, before going to the garden. My husband is not employed but he goes to the village...every day. He comes home late at night when he is dead drunk. And these days if we are lucky, he brings in a piece of soap or some salt. But basically, each of us caters for her own family," says Zahara, referring to herself and her co-wives.

In his drunkenness, Zahara's husband chases them out of the house with death threats. "If it wasn't for my children, I would have run away long ago. But I have to fend for them. He is my husband in name only. I don't want my marriage to be seen to have failed, but he does nothing here apart from drinking," says Zahara ruefully. Five of her children left school because she could not afford the fees.

"I used to have money to buy the basic necessities for my children. Now I have to go to bed before dark because I can't afford to buy paraffin any more. Even soap is expensive," says Zahara, looking at her dirty clothes. "I used to be one of the smartest women here."

"I cannot grow much food for sale," she continues. "I mostly depend on my energy to cultivate a small piece of land which my husband continually mortgages for booze. And the land is also tired. I have been cultivating it for the last 15 years. It now gives me a very small yield." She desperately needs fertiliser, "but where is the money to buy [it]? Sometimes we use dry banana leaves as manure, but this also brings in pests," she says. "I might have borrowed money, but my husband is someone you cannot trust with money. He would either say I stole it from him, or just grab it from me."

Although her father denied her education because she was a girl, she wanted her children to go to school. "My father said it was useless to educate girls since they were going to be married off and become their husbands' property," says Zahara.

Responsibility for children

Ugandan society believes that children belong to the man and that women therefore have no claim over them. There are no national statistics, but very often men father children outside marriage and then refuse to take care of the mothers and children.

Anna Salume, 22, now a mother of two, dropped out of school after she became pregnant. She was in Senior Four. Her parents chased her out of the home, as most parents do in these cases, looking on pregnancy outside marriage as shameful and a major embarrassment for the family. "My parents were so bitter, I think they chased me from home in revenge," says Anna. She went to her grandmother's village in Mbale.

When Anna gave birth to a baby boy, her parents tried to convince the boyfriend he should marry her. He agreed on condition that he first father another child with her. "I accepted because I feared the deadly AIDS", Anna says, "and I didn't want to get involved with another man after having got a baby with this man."

When she conceived a second time, her betrothed, who already had another wife and children, abandoned her and her child. During this time, Anna lost her second baby.

When we met Anna, her case had not been fully settled. FIDA had secured regular help for the child, and they were advising her to look for another man. Mary Mutonyi says such cases are very common. "We normally call on these men and discuss with them about their obligations to the mother and the children they have fathered, after which we try to reach a solution...FIDA cannot force a man to marry a woman. We only give legal advice and we always tell young girls to look for better suitors elsewhere."

Mutonyi says that sometimes the parents' interest is not in getting financial support or custody of the children, but in using the children as weapons to get back at one another after a relationship has broken down. "Sometimes clients come with claims, and only admit that they want to get at their husbands during counselling."

Betty Kancha, a secondary school teacher, separated from her husband two years ago. The husband wanted custody of their three children. When Betty opposed this on the grounds that they were too young to be without her, he refused to pay any maintenance. Betty went to FIDA, who successfully helped her fight for her legal rights. "I was not only allowed to keep the children until they were seven years old, but he was told to give assistance and school fees until they go into his custody," she says.

Harriet Nabawanga of Ntengeru, Mukono District, says she has been unable to solve her problems. One of her daughters, a 15-year-old in Senior One, eloped with an elderly man and did not let her mother know where she had gone. At around the same time, the second daughter had to leave school after becoming pregnant. When she gave birth, the man responsible for the pregnancy abandoned her without giving her any assistance. Harriet herself was raising her nine children single-handedly after separating from her husband, who has neglected them ever since.

"I felt a lot of injustice on me. Men are forcing my children to leave school when they are so young and yet soon after they abandon them," says Harriet. "But I strongly felt there must be some law to protect my children and me." However, she lacked the financial means to engage a lawyer.

Harriet made arrangements to visit FIDA's legal aid clinic in Kampala to see that justice was done. But her endeavours met with opposition from the men in her family who wanted to protect a "fellow man". They pointed out that the other "son-in-law" who had eloped with Harriet's elder daughter had accepted to take the girl as his wife. Harriet never did make it to FIDA.

Women, employment and income

Yoku Masaba has recently started growing coffee again, having abandoned his plantation during the 1980s. With the improved world coffee price and liberalisation of the Uganda coffee industry, things have started to look up for him. At least now, he says, he has a little money to buy himself a new shirt and look decent.

But Masaba does not work on the plantation himself. "My wife tends to the coffee plantation every day and she picks and dries the coffee," he says. Masaba attends to the marketing, and does not consult his wife on how to spend the money earned from coffee sales. "But what can she do? She knows nothing about money, and even then, I am the head of the family and I make all the decisions," says Masaba rather angrily. "She just needs salt and a saucepan for her kitchen."

Masaba is one of those men who think that FIDA is destroying their homes. "I am lucky. I still have full control of my home. My brother's wife comes home late because she sells in the market and demands that he help her with the work since she is tired. How can I go to the kitchen or tend to a crying baby? What is a woman for?" asks Masaba in disbelief. His grandparents knew what a woman's work was, he says, and he can't change customs.

Nambozo, Masaba's wife, says she has no choice but to accept her situation. "My husband paid a heavy bride price before we married. He owns me as part of his property, and if I complain, he reminds me of the bride price," she says.

An ox plough and pesticides would help Nambozo farm more efficiently, instead of depending on the hoe and God's mercy. "Most of us want to expand our incomes but we have no capital. I want to borrow money but I fear that I may not be able to pay it back. Even then, my husband will just take it from me."

In contrast to Masaba, Ssalongo has come to value his wife's capacity to earn an income. Along with thousands of men in the civil service, he has recently been retrenched. These cuts are the latest in a series of stringent measures taken under the structural adjustment programme. Unable to find alternative employment

Small amounts of money earned through selling vegetables in the market help reduce women's dependence on their husbands.

in the town, Ssalongo returned to his village, Mbigi.

In the past Ssalongo had criticised his wife, Nalongo, for joining a women's group, but now he appreciates her decision. She is a farmer belonging to a group called Tukolerewamu ("Let's work together"), which has 10 members. They grow vegetables and raise chickens for sale.

"In addition, each of us contributes 2,000 shillings [US$2.15] every month for one of the members, so that she can do something substantial. Some of the members use the money for school fees, which otherwise would have been impossible," says Nalongo. "I had my turn in June and I bought material for making tablecloths to get some extra income."

The government has had new roads made in the area, and now people come to buy their products which are later sold in Kampala. "The roads are better now than in the past, although they are not as good as those in Kampala," Nalongo says. "We work in turns, each woman taking two days to attend to the chickens."

The group was formed after FIDA personnel went to visit their area, urging the women to start income-generating activities, instead of being dependent on their husbands. Ssalongo remembers: "I thought these FIDA people were crazy. How could they tell my wife to start working? That would mean my children going hungry because she would not be here to cook. I thought it was the beginning of the disintegration of my home. The idea of her being away from home made me mad." But since Nalongo has started bringing in money, Ssalongo's attitude has changed drastically. During the harvest period, she earns between 6,000 and 20,000 shillings (US$6.50-21.50) a month and the occasional tray of eggs.

Other initiatives

In Mbale, the Uganda Women's Finance and Credit Trust (UWFCT) was set up in 1984 in conjunction with FIDA as a pilot project on credit and the law. "Whenever we go out to visit the rural areas, we encourage women to start income-generating activities with the help of UWFCT finance," says Mutonyi.

The goal is to emancipate women economically and improve their status by increasing their access to legal and credit services, together with general education on matters of law and finance. "We hope to achieve this by providing legal, credit and savings services to women," says Grace Mutenyo, the project manager. "If women have to become economically independent, they should have access to financial institutions to lend them money on favourable terms." Betty Luba, the UWFCT credit officer, says that some of the groups they have funded have been successful. "After paying the loans, some of these women start individual income-generating activities," she says.

Activities of this kind have increased since the NRM came to power. Ntulume Village Women's Development Association (NVWDA), for example, was formed on 6 September 1988 with the aim of mobilising and training women in income-generating activities, so as to improve their standard of living.

NVWDA's members were concerned about the health risks to women who, when menstruating, traditionally made do with bits of rag or toilet paper. To encourage better hygiene, and as a means of earning money, they decided to establish a group making sanitary towels. But demand has been low. "Since there were so many women around, [we hoped] we would have a ready market for our products," says Cissy Nyarwa, head of the association. "But this is not forthcoming. People are not yet used to our towels."

The group also grows flowers and seedlings for hedges, and teaches women how to make various handicrafts for sale. Nyarwa says they still lack technical know-how to help them improve their products but that the group has spurred other initiatives. "After [we formed] this association, other women also started forming their own associations, and they are actively involved in things like poultry, piggeries, bee-keeping and farming," she says.

However, Winnie Kibuuka says that she has tried without much success to organise women into groups to start income-generating activities. "The problem is that we do not have the capital. Even then, the handicrafts that we make are not very marketable. And when we see you people from Kampala coming here," she says with a smile, "we think you have brought us something to help us start a business."

She adds that farming "is our only hope." The President told them to grow vanilla and flowers as a quick way of making money. "But vanilla takes too long to grow," she says. And recently, the Minister of Agriculture, Victoria Sekitoleko, said that growing vanilla was uneconomical. "People are confused", she says, "about what to do and who to believe."

Gaining ground

FIDA's work in encouraging income-generating activities among women is progressing only slowly and remains of secondary importance compared with their advisory and campaigning work. This is where the organisation is able to use its professional expertise most effectively.

The extent of the task that confronts FIDA is enormous: the queues of women waiting for advice in the legal clinics do not get any smaller and the obstacles to be overcome at the political and social level remain considerable. But gradually, women are becoming aware of their rights and demanding redress for the wrongs they have suffered.

Betty Kancha, a beneficiary of FIDA's assistance, is convinced that women are gaining ground. "The opponents of FIDA should well know that trying to fight it is only fighting a losing battle, because today more and more women are getting enlightened about their legal rights, with the full backing of the government."

Weathering the Crisis

Drought, structural adjustment and community development in Zimbabwe

Recurrent drought and the stringencies of Zimbabwe's structural adjustment programme are jeopardising development work undertaken by the Organisation of Rural Associations for Progress (ORAP) with the people of Midlands and Matabeleland North and South. Residents of these provinces describe to **Farayi A Chimbindi** their disaffection with central government, their productive achievements in difficult circumstances, and their fears and hopes for the future. Photographs by **Calvin Duodo**.

As you drive south from Harare, you could be forgiven for thinking that Zimbabwe is a land endowed with limitless resources. Forests and fields stretch out from each side of the road, and there is little evidence of human habitation. It is only the barbed wire fences that hint at the reality behind the impression.

Zimbabwe is indeed a sparsely populated country, having an area of some 390,000 sq km and a population of only 10 million, which results in a density of only 27 people per sq km. But there are still great inequalities, especially between the black majority and the white minority. All the rich land we have passed is fenced off by large-scale commercial farmers, most of whom are white. Commercial farmers number just 4,500, yet they own 50% of

Zimbabwe's productive land—the best land, with the most reliable levels of rainfall. Everyone else ekes out an existence in the communal lands. This grossly unequal distribution of land explains why, despite impressive gains in food production since the early 1980s, almost a million rural families remain vulnerable to malnutrition.

Once we reach the communal areas, the harsh reality of life for the one million smallholders and their families is brought sharply into focus. The signs of poverty are all too clear: the soil is dusty and visibly tired, crops are sparse, houses are in disrepair, roads are full of potholes. Pushed off the most fertile land by decades of colonial law-making, people living in communal areas can expect a life no better than that in many poor African countries.

While Zimbabwe's per capita GNP, at 5,200 Zimbabwean dollars (US$650), defines it as a middle-income country, the greatest proportion of that income is concentrated in urban areas and large-scale commercial farms. People living in communal areas have a life expectancy of 56 years, although the infant mortality rate is fairly low at 59 per 1,000 live births. Only 36% of the population have access to safe water, and 42% to sanitation [1].

Poor farmers—especially women—also suffer because infrastructural support, irrigation, and investment generally, is concentrated in the commercial farming areas, while more marginal and remote regions are overlooked. Commercial farmers benefit from access to credit, often on subsidised terms, while small producers are typically excluded from credit markets. This denies them access to other productive inputs, such as fertiliser, seeds, oxen and farming implements.

In 1991 and 1992, Zimbabwe was hit by a severe drought. Harvests failed completely, and the cattle population was decimated. At the same time, Zimbabwe was embarking upon its Economic Structural Adjustment Programme. Prices shot up, food became scarce and employment fell as the government retrenched many workers. Medical and school fees were reintroduced and escalated rapidly. School fees are now 500 dollars per pupil per year (US$62.5), three times the national minimum monthly wage [2].

The rural population suffered most. The drought severely

impaired people's ability to survive and many became dependent on food aid. As unemployment hit the towns, remittances to rural areas also dropped, and urban migrants returned to their villages, seeking support from extended families already stretched to breaking point.

A field of your own

Rural households in Zimbabwe are increasingly female-headed. Many women work their fields for several months of the year but go to the towns after harvest to be with their husbands. They return to prepare the land in September, ahead of the rains that usually start in November. Besides undertaking the bulk of agricultural work, they are responsible for a multiplicity of other roles—childrearing, cooking, fetching water and firewood, and marketing food staples—vital to household food security.

"In the morning", recounts one woman in Gwanda North (a district south of Bulawayo), "before the children go to school, five of us go and fetch water. In the afternoon we go to collect firewood. I have a small garden where I grow vegetables that I sell. After selling them in the township, I go home and cook. It's winter now, so at least the workload is reduced, without the ploughing."

Yet women are systematically denied access to productive resources. In communal areas, where 70% of the population live, all land is state land; it is only under customary law that local people own land. The smallholder has no legal title and therefore cannot use it as collateral for institutional credit. In addition, customary practices do not allow women to own land. Although, since independence from Britain in 1980, the government has legally affirmed women's basic right to land ownership, cultural and economic constraints often combine to deny them effective ownership and control.

Zimbabwe is a patrilineal society. Only men are allocated land by chiefs. Whether or not a woman is allowed a field for her own use and control depends on her husband's goodwill, and he may withdraw this right at any time. But women do have the right to own livestock and to use grazing land for their animals.

A divorced woman automatically loses access to any land she

has been cultivating as she is required to leave the family home and return to her original home. A widow may take over her late husband's land, but this may be disputed by her in-laws. The practice of marrying one of the husband's brothers is gradually dying out.

"If you have a field of your own, you can use the money as you like, without anyone controlling you. You are not like a child," says Tenjiwe Moyo, the youngest member of the Zama Women's Garden Project in Tsholotsho (a district in Matabeleland South). "Having a field of my own is important—very important, because when I am in need of something I can use my own money without asking my husband. If a relative comes or my children want something, I just use my money."

Women and men do not always agree on what to grow on the land. "My husband wants to grow maize mostly", says Agnes Sibanda of Silobela, "but I want to have a field for growing peanuts. We rely on peanut butter during the dry months for relish."

Women's rights to land ownership do not receive wholehearted support from the government. President Robert Mugabe recently responded to a suggestion that property belonging to a couple should be registered in both names by saying: "I cannot have it that property that is family property should be registered in two names. If a woman wanted property in her own right, why did she get married in the first place? [3]."

"Some women would agree with him. "It is every woman's pride to be married," says 53-year-old Rosina Nkomo. "The husband is always the head of the family—even the Bible says that. I think some of the people who are saying that women are equal to men want to destroy our culture."

Matabeles under siege

The Matabele people live in the Matabeleland South and North and the Midlands provinces of Zimbabwe, mainly in the communal areas. These are areas of regularly recurring drought, where the economy is particularly dependent on livestock, the majority of inhabitants being settled pastoralists. Underdevelopment, scattered and remote communities, and environmental degradation characterise all three provinces, and these factors have led to a high level of food insecurity which is the greatest constraint to development.

The Matabeles are one of Zimbabwe's two broad ethnic and linguistic groups. Outnumbered four to one by the majority Shonas, the Matabeles, an offshoot of the Zulus of South Africa, held military power over the Shonas a century ago. After independence, political power shifted to the Shonas, which led to the civil war of the early 1980s. A Unity Accord was signed in 1987 between President Mugabe, representing the predominantly Shona ZANU (PF), and Joshua Nkomo, the leader of the Matabele-dominated ZAPU. This has helped to balance political representation between the two groups at the national level.

The civil war has, nonetheless, left its mark. "War disrupted everything—schools, hospitals, dip tanks. Our culture was broken. There was no respect," says Josephine Dube, a widow, whose husband was forced to dig his own grave before being shot by soldiers in 1983; she is now a ruling party political commissioner for Matabeleland South. Another woman, who declined to be named, says: "We have now all joined the ruling party, not for the love of it, but for survival. We like to forgive but not forget the past."

Many feel that they are being ignored by the Harare-based government, dominated by Shonas. Josephine Dube comments: "I don't think the Smith government would have allowed the wanton cutting-down of trees now taking place in Pumula, Dibutibu and Nchaeli. All our grazing land is now naked. How can the government allow a private company to cut *mukwa* [indigenous hardwood] and teak without consulting us. These are our trees, and we are getting nothing in return."

Rhoda Khumalo, aged 63 and a voluntary community mobiliser with the Organisation of Rural Associations for Progress (ORAP) agrees. "We just don't expect much from the government," she says. "All we want is enabling power to help ourselves."

Even some government workers hold similar views. One in Tsholotsho, who prefers not to be named, says: "It seems the government wants to develop the areas around Harare, not us out here. See how they are dilly-dallying about the Zambezi Water Project. This is the only long-term solution to our crisis."

This proposed project, to install a 450-km pipeline carrying water from the Zambezi down into Matabeleland, is seen by many as the potential saviour of the area, the only way of tackling the chronic shortage of water.

The central government's role in contributing to development in the area comes in for harsh criticism. Education is a major source of concern. "Before independence you knew that if your son completed Form Four, he was sure to get a decent job," complains Lot Nkomo, a blacksmith at ORAP's Stanmore Development Centre in Gwanda (the provincial capital of Matabeleland South). "Today even university graduates roam the streets or just waste away drinking beer with us here in the countryside."

"Some of our Form Four pupils cannot compare to our Standard Six pupils during Smith's time," says Veronica Moyo, whose husband was a village head killed by soldiers during the civil war. "What can you expect when they are taught by someone who has also failed his Form Four?" she asks, referring to the fact that as part of the government's Growth with Equity programme in the early 1980s, hundreds of "temporary" unqualified teachers were recruited to fill the new schools that were built.

Inflation is also a problem blamed on the government. "Cement used to be very cheap," says Lot Nkomo. "Today, a [50 kg] bag of cement will cost you 40 dollars [US$5]. How can we build better homes? Only the rich can afford things these days."

Evangelista Ndlovu says that because the soil is exhausted, using fertiliser is the only way of achieving a reasonable yield. "But who can afford it today? We hear that a tonne of maize [20 bags] costs 900 dollars [US$112.50], which is the cost of sending your child to boarding school. Most of us produce only five bags or so if the season is good."

David Nkomo contrasts the pre- and post-colonial periods succinctly: "They used to harass us at the District Commissioner's Office when we went to get birth certificates. We would bow our heads and salute the *inkosi* [white district

In the drought, many water sources in Matabeleland have dried up completely.

commissioner]. That was very humiliating. Nowadays, most of the time they tell you to come back next week because there is no paper or the person in charge is away."

Not everyone is so critical. "It's very easy to forget", points out Sipiladzima Dube, who chairs the Tsholotsho council, "that we were treated like slaves in our own country. Today, we have the dignity of a people and can walk freely. The government has built schools and clinics nearer to the people. I think that is a very positive development."

Drought, economics and survival

Drought is nothing new to Zimbabwe. The drought of 1991-92 was the most devastating in a century, but the rains failed again catastrophically in 1994. Agnes Mtunzi, a 62-year-old widow, says this drought is the worst one she has ever seen. "The last time we had slightly-above rains was in 1980," she recalls, visibly distraught. "The government has not helped us." She had been trying to recover from the 1991-92 drought, which wiped out her herd of cattle, when the drought of 1994 struck. "I had 14 cattle", she says, "and they all died in the 1992 drought. I have no draught power so I only use my hands to work the land. Being a widow I don't have anyone to help me."

The rains should have continued until April, but not a drop fell after January. According to local councillor Jeremiah Langa, of the Pansikwe area of Filabusi, harvests were only a tenth of their usual yields and even drought-resistant crops were affected. "As if the lack of rains were not enough, mice ate up the little food there was and frost wiped out all the vegetables," says Langa, who complains that his appeals to the government have gone unanswered.

The combined effects of the drought and the structural adjustment programme have left many people unable to survive as before. Remittances from migrant labourers have dropped, fertiliser prices have sky-rocketed, and animal draught power is in short supply, as donkeys and cattle have either died or are too weak to pull ploughs.

People have been forced to pursue alternative survival strategies. One of these is gold panning. A "gold belt" runs east-west from Filabusi to Bulawayo in Matabeleland South, and Gwanda has grown into a small mining town. Illegal panning in the waterways is rife and is accelerating the loss of fragile soils.

"Gold panning has replaced crop farming here," says Jeremiah Langa. "The Insiza River is now an eyesore and every day people converge with picks and pans searching for gold." The river bed and banks have been scarred by pits and trenches, some as wide as basketball courts, some several metres deep. "Community leaders trying to educate people about the environmental damage are accused of being insensitive to the poverty people face," says Langa.

Four Zs and a Q

Founded in 1980 by a group made up predominantly of teachers, clergy and civic leaders, ORAP has mobilised communities through five basic principles, popularly known as the Four Zs and a Q:

Zigoge (mobilise yourself)
Zenzele (do it yourself)
Ziqhatshe (sustain yourself)
Zimele (be independent)
Qogelela (build up resources)

According to founding member and chief executive Sithembiso Nyoni, "ORAP mobilises people to do their own development the way they see it and know best, emphasising the use of local resources, because that way rural people value their land, culture and themselves. ORAP was conceived to develop an alternative to the prevalent top-down prescriptions and remedies for development. Aid must not be the basis for development. Rural people have a wealth of skills, knowledge and wisdom. We should promote the livelihood of rural people in every way possible, because unless we uplift the rural population we will never have a nation."

Nyoni is a persuasive and charismatic person. She was among five women worldwide who won the alternative Nobel Prize— the Right Livelihood Award—in 1993 for their positive contributions in situations of crisis. The award was given in recognition of Nyoni's—and ORAP's—efforts in motivating more than a million people to choose their own development path and for their effective response to the 1991-92 drought. Nyoni ploughed back the US$50,000 prize money into the organisation.

ORAP has developed more than 150 different types of activity in household technology, agriculture and drought relief. Social structures and administrative structures are one and the same thing. The primary unit is the family which, together with neighbouring households, debates development issues affecting it and tries to come up with solutions. The family unit is also responsible for mobilising the human and financial resources necessary to achieve these solutions. Next comes the group, comprising several family units, which discusses and shares ideas and experiences.

One group is gathered at the home of Rhoda Khumalo. Like other mobilisers we have met, Khumalo is warm and friendly, speaks articulately about the problems of the area, and is quick in suggesting solutions.

"We have a serious water and food crisis here. We started meetings yesterday on how to beat the crisis," she says as she introduces us to the 16 women sitting in a circle in her spotlessly clean kitchen. They are busy making straw hats, and carry on their discussion while they work.

"We have decided that each household should contribute 20 or 15 dollars (US$2-2.50), depending on how much they can afford. We look at the family size to see how many kilograms of maize meal they need to survive. On average, two 50-kg bags of maize meal will carry the family through the month. Old ladies or widows, we have agreed, should contribute 15 dollars. Other, less poor, families will contribute 20 dollars each," says Khumalo.

Most of the women say they will raise their contributions to the drought relief fund by selling tomatoes. "But our tomatoes have been hit by a severe frost this week, so we have decided to sell the little that is available, but we will not use the money to buy maize meal," says 59-year-old Levy Siziba. "If we can raise, say, 200 dollars (US$25) each from selling tomatoes, we will put that money together and one of us will go to Bulawayo to buy straw. I bought straw for 10 dollars and made eight hats. The hats sell very fast in Bulawayo at 20 to 25 dollars each (US$2.50-3) so that way we will generate more money to buy maize meal. We are now training others to make the hats. I can make a nice hat in an hour or two."

Turning to the water crisis, Khumalo says that the villages around have only one source left. "All our other wells have dried up. We have agreed to take turns to fetch water. If five can fetch water in the mornings, others will do the same in the afternoons and evenings to allow the water to accumulate in the well." Should the water level become lower still, Khumalo says they will meet to agree on further methods of rationing the water. "Maybe each family will have one day or two in a week when they can fetch water."

What if the well dries out completely? "We will dig the river banks. This happened in the last drought. Below those sands there is some water. So, together with all able-bodied men, we will dig."

At the home of Rhoda Khumalo in Gwanda North, a women's group makes hats for sale in Bulawayo while discussing the food and water crisis. Proceeds will go to the community's drought relief fund.

When there is a need for common representation, as is often the case, the group takes the matter to the body known as the "umbrella", made up of representatives of groups in a particular area. The district association is the representative body of all the umbrellas in the district. The executives of these associations form the board of ORAP, which advises the organisation on how to address the issues raised by their communities. Upon recommendation from the associations, the advisory board can employ people, especially mobilisers and fieldworkers. Together with ORAP staff, the advisory board makes policy for the organisation.

Collectivism: good or bad?

Many people want to join ORAP. "I have just moved into this area," says Amanda Ngwenya in Gwanda North. "I would very much like to join ORAP. We are always buying vegetables from them." Veronica Moyo complains that while many people in her village west of Tsholotsho were eager to join ORAP and start income-generating projects, "the [ORAP] mobilisers have not responded to us. We have asked them to come and help us but they don't come." ORAP finds that it is unable to keep up with all the requests for assistance that it receives.

ORAP is not universally popular. "I believe in doing things on my own," says a young man who claims to have been a freedom fighter in the liberation war. "To me, ORAP is a socialist organisation, but we all know that socialism does not work. When everybody is in charge, nobody will be responsible."

This suspicion of "socialism" or collectivism is common. "They built a grinding mill here and it closed," says an official at the Tsholotsho district administrator's office. "It isn't working because some spare part is missing. If the grinding mill belonged to one businessman, it would be working today."

Memories of the operations of the Fifth Brigade remain vivid: this was the North Korean-trained, predominantly Shona brigade, deployed to quell armed dissent in Matabeleland after independence. "Since the Fifth Brigade operations," says one 54-year-old amputee, "I have learned that it is not safe to belong to organisations. You get killed for nothing. Many people were killed here. I will attend rallies if called by the government, but I will not be an active member of any organisation any more."

Government officials complain that ORAP does not try to coordinate or consult with them, operating completely independently. "All other NGOs such as the Freedom from Hunger Campaign, the Catholics and Oxfam first come and talk to us, but ORAP just goes straight to the villagers," says one official. ORAP itself claims to work closely with the local authorities.

"We no longer beg"

After a 100-km drive from Bulawayo, travelling northwest to Tsholotsho, a bumpy road leads us to Mhlabangubo School in Chief Nqoya's territory. The uninspiring view of parched plains, where emaciated goats and donkeys graze on thorny bushes, is abruptly broken by the sight of vegetables flourishing. This plot of land, about half a hectare in size, is Zama Women's Garden Project. *Zama* means "try it" in Ndebele.

The project has been operating for well over a decade. "We started after the war in 1981. The war had disrupted everything. Schools, hospitals and dip tanks were closed," Zama member Mandiya Ndlovu, aged 61, recalls.

Elina Ncube, aged 49, is a widow and mother of eight. She is also a mobiliser for ORAP. "Before the amnesty in 1987, we couldn't meet," she says. "We want to forget about the past. There isn't much we can do about it. ORAP was our fortune. They came and started bringing us together. We talked. It was a meeting of the brains. We wanted respect for our culture restored. Things like you coming to ask my daughter out in my presence, something unheard of in our culture, had become common during the war," she says.

Elizabeth Ndlovu, 51, a former head of the pre-school at the garden, says: "We have come full circle. This association has helped us culturally. We now do things the way we used to in the old days. When a neighbour is sick we collect firewood, fetch water and clean their homes. We help each other, but we couldn't do that in the war. Even in the fields we help each other with ploughing and weeding. All this we owe to the cooperative. We are trying to help ourselves. We sell vegetables within the community and raise money for school fees, for grinding our maize and other things.... ORAP gave us education. We can do things on our own. We no longer beg. We are independent."

Forty-year-old Anastasia Ngwenya, ORAP's field coordinator in Tsholotsho, explains that she is responsible for some 2,000 members in the district. "Before setting up this garden, women had small gardens along the stream banks," she says. "We used to walk long distances to fetch water and our vegetables were from time to time destroyed by roaming cattle and goats. This collective garden is secure. Water is readily available and all year round. We buy seeds and sprays collectively. We don't use chemical fertilisers, only cattle manure. Fertilisers are expensive, and vegetables grown on them are tasteless."

At 68, Zama treasurer Francisca Sithole is the oldest member. She says projects like Zama could not be undertaken in the past "because we didn't have the knowledge." The group's secretary, 38-year-old Gezepi Ndlovu, asserts: "This project came out of us. We met and we talked about our needs. The only contribution by the government is the extension worker."

All the members are positive about the extension worker. "If it were not for him, most of our vegetables would have been eaten by pests. He knows the right sprays to use. We give him the money and he buys the chemicals for us."

"The project is ours not ORAP's," says Elizabeth Ndlovu. "We have now saved 3,000 dollars [US$375] in our common fund. This money we have in the past used for erecting a wall around the well for pipes, and we also bought an additional hand-pumped borehole which has eased our burden greatly. We are saving on average 100 dollars [US$12.50] a month," she claims.

The 34 project members, who include two men, each have six beds and grow a range of vegetables. Each member sets aside two beds from which produce is sold, the proceeds all going into the project's common fund.

"Our husbands are very supportive of this project. When I am away, my husband comes to water the garden," says chairperson Love Ndlovu. "They are happy because they too gain from this garden. Now, instead of the men, we are the ones who help out paying school fees. They often ask us for money for a beer. This year we are buying grain because of the drought."

Tenjiwe Moyo, aged 27, joined in 1991. Her husband is unemployed, as are many of the other men in the community. "I have three children, all going to school," she says. "They need food, soap, uniforms and much of that comes from this garden."

Some of the men, although positive, see the garden primarily as a useful supplement to their livelihoods. "I cannot say my family and I are dependent on the garden," says Jacob Nkomo.

"But it certainly helps our diet, especially in the dry season. The garden has relieved us from the fate of eating dried vegetables. But as you know, you can't eat vegetables every day. I still have to buy meat."

"I think this is a wonderful project. It has improved our diet," says Sipho Moyo. "Our cows are dry because these pastures are dry, so we can't have milk. So that's where the garden comes in handy. I don't think the issue is whether or not we as husbands are dependent on our wives. A family is like a company. Each member should contribute towards improving our life."

Tenjiwe says that working with older women is enriching. "They give us tips about how to maintain a happy family. We sometimes argue over changing lifestyles and gender issues, but it all ends well. We want to use our savings to open kiosks. This will enable us to sell more of our produce, particularly at Tsholotsho Business Centre, which is nearby. We are also seriously considering expanding our garden. We have children who can help."

There is spare land still available at Zama. New members can join if they pay 38 dollars (US$4.75). "This is because we have already developed the infrastructure," says Francisca Sithole. "We want to set up village markets. We could set up a chain of wholesalers in the country, selling processed agricultural products, such as cooking oil from our vegetables and sunflower seeds."

It is difficult to gauge the sustainability of this project, as information on expenditure and income is very scant, and the level of ORAP's inputs is also difficult to measure. What is clear, however, is that the members believe in it strongly. It provides a vital, if small, income. There is a high degree of interest in improving the garden and the marketing of produce. Improvements will necessarily be small and incremental because of the lack of capital and the small size and limited spending power of local markets for the produce.

Could other groups successfully copy Zama? Love Ndlovu is doubtful: "It is very difficult to replicate this project. It is not easy to achieve community involvement. That is the key to the success we enjoy."

Better granaries, traditional seeds

"A lot of food in Zimbabwe is...lost post-harvest", says Mpiliso Ndiweni, head of ORAP's Food Security and Environment Unit. "That could be, according to statistics, as high as 20% in some cases." To keep out the pests that devour the stored crops, ORAP has designed improved granaries, using bricks and cement.

One of the 17 granaries built so far is at Mavava village, 7 km from the Tsholotsho Centre. With a capacity of 60 bags (5.5 tonnes) of grain, it is situated in the homestead of Rosina Nkomo, aged 53, who speaks enthusiastically of its benefits. "We can store our maize, millet or sorghum for years and it will be clean. All the family has to do is bring their grain and we record the quantity, and then they can always come and collect the amount they require."

The granaries range in size from a single family granary capable of storing 23 bags, to the district granaries that can carry 800 bags. ORAP provides the cement, while communities make the bricks and hire a builder. "Before, we had a granary made out of mud and poles," says David Nkomo, a father of eight. "But our maize was eaten by rats, or even got stolen overnight. This is a better granary. It's secure, and the maize doesn't rot." It also has a compartment for storing dried vegetables.

The granaries are built under ORAP's home improvement scheme, whose beneficiaries include Sipho Ndlovu and his family in Gwanda. A five-roomed brick and thatch house is near completion. "Even if I worked for 10 years I could never afford this house," says Sipho. "Even motorists driving past stop to admire [it]."

Kitchens have also been improved. Walls and surfaces are coated with wood ash, dried goat manure or other natural substances. "There are certain types of indigenous tree in Matabeleland that people have always used, which provide a very fine ash-like dust. Therefore, weevils cannot stay in there," explains David Nkomo.

These ideas seem to be spreading fast. Similar improved granaries and kitchens can be seen in Silobela in the Midlands. "The granaries ensure that there is food security within the homes

Under ORAP's home improvement scheme, kitchen walls coated with pest-resistant natural materials help improve food security.

and in much more decentralised areas," says Ndiweni. "We expect that once we have granaries in as many homes as possible, it will be much less costly to move food to areas of need."

He says that the cost of transporting food is now higher than the cost of the food itself. "Through the years, ORAP has been selling food at cost price to villagers. Our only subsidy was transport, [the cost of] which has shot up drastically."

Along with pest-free storage facilities, traditional seeds are vital to food security, ORAP believes. "Most farmers", says Ndiweni with regret, "have moved into growing maize and that is mainly the hybrid seed, which is dependent on expensive chemical fertilisers and requires a lot of rain. Yet this area is more suitable for the traditional drought-resistant small grains, millet and sorghum." He admits that public tastes have shifted to maize, "but we are concerned about nutrition and production. So we are working with various other parties interested in bringing back small grain production."

It is clear that ORAP will have a struggle changing views. In the communal areas, small grains are widely used for brewing *utshwala* (traditional beer) and sometimes for making porridge, but this means strenuous extra work for the women. "First, there is the back-breaking pounding, using the mortar and pestle to remove the outer husks," explains Rhoda Khumalo. "This is followed by winnowing and then more laborious grinding using a grinding stone. You kneel on the floor to crush the grain and this takes many hours to yield flour to make just one meal."

Another woman, Queen Mpofu, from Tsholotsho, says: "My children hate porridge made out of millet. They like the white maize. In fact, when I prepare porridge with millet, the following day they often complain of stomach ache. I personally like the taste, but preparing the flour is very hard work." Organisations like the Environment and Development Association are introducing hammer mills to ease the work, but even then the cost of grinding small grains into flour is higher than it is for maize.

Men are more positive about small grains, saying that the yields are better. "They are also very easy to store as they hardly get eaten by pests. You can store millet for years," says Jacob Nkomo, in charge of the Mavava grinding mill. "But I think if the Grain Marketing Board [GMB] can offer higher prices for small grains, more farmers would increase production. Now they fetch very little, if the GMB buys at all."

Development centres under threat

"We regard this centre as truly ours, although ORAP helped us set it up," says an elderly villager. "It used to be a lively forum for discussion and exchanging of information by the community. Certainly things have gone down a lot."

Built by ORAP, with community contributions of labour, materials, skills and sometimes money, Vusisizwe Development Centre in Silobela communal area in the Midlands is one of eight ORAP-assisted development centres in the three provinces. Standing in impoverished surroundings, it boasts an administration block with 11 offices, a community hall and a pre-school. It also houses a village market and a sewing centre.

Because of high unemployment in the country, especially among school leavers, the centre has from the outset placed an emphasis on training the youth. "A lot of young people were

New granaries, built with ORAP's help, enable families and communities to store grain safely for several years.

trained in building, even as the centre got built," says the administrator, 25-year-old Aleck Nkiwane. "We have facilities for training in carpentry, blacksmithing and in general repair of such things as boreholes and domestic and agricultural implements." Tinsmithing and sewing were two other types of training offered in the 1980s.

Nowadays there is little activity going on. The centre is seriously short of money. ORAP's resources from donors are in decline and, as result of the structural adjustment programme, the government is reducing public spending. Local people cannot be expected to pay more either: with declining harvests their ability to contribute financially is severely restricted. The centre is dwindling into a ghost facility.

According to Nkiwane, the centre operated at near capacity between 1983 and 1987. "We had many youths training in blacksmithing and carpentry. But because of the civil war, people began to withdraw from the centre, giving the opportunity to vandals to steal building materials and some carpentry and blacksmithing tools."

He claims that serious reconstruction of the centre began in

November 1993, a month after he took up the post of administrator. "We are renovating dormitories and repainting the centre. Our target is to acquire tools for the various training disciplines and attract skilled trainers."

"The water crisis has crippled our operations," says Nkiwane. Part of the reconstruction involved the drilling of two boreholes. One has a hand pump which is in working order, the other a huge windmill which has broken down. The windmill is not pumping water "because one of its sails is not moving well", according to Nkiwane. "It has never worked for two straight months without a breakdown. We are lucky that the installers are repairing on a guarantee basis because we don't have any skilled people locally to attend to it." The breakdown teams from the installers have driven three times from Kwekwe to repair the windmill but each time it has broken down again as soon as they leave. "We are expecting them again next week," he says.

However, the one functioning borehole is a lifeline for the community. Simelene Dube, aged 32, with a four-month-old son strapped to her back and accompanied by her sister, says they come from a village 1.5 km away to fetch water from the centre. They drive a cart, drawn by donkeys, which carries 20 litres of water.

"Our cry is for more boreholes," she says, adding that she is digging a well at her home. According to her, the water shortage is behind the seeming decay of the centre. "I attended a pre-school course here on cookery. That was some time back when the centre was still very lively," she explains. "The centre is still useful for us because we collect our water and fertilisers here."

James Gundhla, 38, a tractor driver with the government tillage unit in the area, is not so sure: "This centre is not much use to the community. Look at it: there is nothing happening here." He says there are a few secondary school pupils who board there. "And we park our tractors here," he adds sarcastically.

The Centre was meant to be a forum for the local community to discuss and work out development strategies. But a local nurse says that it has turned into a place of worship for Jehovah's Witnesses. The decay of these ORAP centres, once hailed as "development points", is echoed by women in Matabeleland South.

At another ORAP-aided centre in Mzingwane near Gwanda, Nelly Sibanda, 71, says: "[The centre] used to help us. Now it doesn't. We now use the centre for meetings only." She says that villagers used to work there in return for money, seeds or cement. "Now we just work. The men have stopped coming because they want money."

"You have to understand that the drought and political disturbances have been the culprits," claims Nkiwane. "To a great extent, I would say that the development centres are still serving their communities." But he says that to attract qualified artisans as instructors to his remote centre will be difficult. "We have to offer competitive pay and provide them with good housing with electricity and tap water."

Present problems, future hopes

Water is the most urgent need in Matabeleland and the Midlands. Jephat Mtetwa, a 55-year-old storekeeper in Kezi, bewails the situation. "Look everywhere.... Can you see any livestock? They have all gone to a dam which is far far away. They also need water. The situation is pathetic." The common cry is for more boreholes, whereas politicians tend to see deliverance through bigger dam projects.

"Government ministries, politicians, churches and all non-governmental organisations should put their heads together to save our desperate provinces from their water woes by tapping the water from the mighty Zambezi River," says Welshman Mabhena, governor of Matabeleland North. "Because of recurring droughts, water tables in most of Matabeleland have lowered. Most boreholes have not served well. Water programmes should concentrate on dam construction rather than borehole drilling."

Some ordinary people agree. One woman in Tsholotsho says: "I think ORAP should concentrate on building us big dams. These boreholes can dry up very easily." Agnes Mtunzi has also lost faith in boreholes. "Most of our pumps have broken down, and some boreholes have dried up. We now have to make do with one borehole which for some people is 7 km away."

A government worker in Tsholotsho complains: "ORAP is

distracting people from demanding that the government develop this area. We don't need small vegetable gardens. That is petty. If there is a big dam, we can all grow and make big money."

After disclosing that his ministry has secured a loan from the Fund for Arab Economic Development for the purpose of drilling boreholes in communal and resettlement areas, Boniface Ndimande, permanent secretary in the Ministry of Lands, Agriculture and Water Development, says that the government has plans to construct a medium-sized dam in every district. "Once the financial situation becomes normal, we should be able to satisfy the demand for irrigation at a faster rate than we are able to at present."

The government's failure to include the proposed Zambezi Water Project in the 1994/95 budget has raised fears among local politicians that it is not committed to its construction. Dumiso Dabengwa, home affairs minister and chairman of the Matabeleland Zambezi Water Trust, which will administer the project, says: "The government has thrown back the ball to the local community to seek funds from both external and local donors, while a feasibility study by Swedish consultants is being held."

Unemployment and the withdrawal of public services are major causes of concern. "If only the government could employ our men. Unemployment and retrenchment are bad. If it's a people's government, how can they reintroduce hospital and school fees?" asks Elizabeth Ndlovu. "I suspect that the high failure rate among schoolchildren is deliberate because the government knows that if they pass they cannot employ them.... This is very bad."

Statistics released by the Ministry of Labour in July 1994 show that a total of 20,710 workers were laid off between January 1991 and April 1994, and that unemployment rose from 37.2% in 1990 to 44% in the first quarter of 1993.

Sipho Ndlovu, who is 45, worked for many years in Bulawayo as a cook. "When my employers left for South Africa in 1978, I came back home...I stayed with relatives in Bulawayo, but it was very difficult to get any job. I have given up all hope of getting employed. More so now with thousands of young and better educated people to compete against."

Albert Ncube is 25, although he looks as if he is in his late 30s. "I completed my 'O' Levels eight years ago", he says, "but I have never been able to find a job. I stayed in Harare for six months seeking any form of employment. I left because I had become a bother to my uncle with whom I lived. I used to sell sweets, oranges and cigarettes on the streets and we would be arrested by the police." City by-laws in Zimbabwe forbid the selling of goods on the street.

"I am hopeful that if the Zambezi Water Project begins I may get a job. They will need lots of people to dig the ground for the water pipeline," he says. If nothing comes up in the next two years, he plans to go to South Africa.

People's hopes for development are simple, if ambitious. "Development means a clean home," says Nellie Sibanda, 36, and a mother of five. "We want to have clean toilets, running water, fuel and electricity." She adds: "I want to be able to pay fees for my daughter to attend a good school, not these secondary schools here where the majority of pupils fail."

"Look at yourself," says Elina Ncube. "You are wearing nice clothes and shoes. That is also what we want."

But it is not only material development that preoccupies people. Mindful of the troubles of the past, Elizabeth Ndlovu says: "We want to have self-respect and respect for others, to be able to accommodate differing viewpoints. We should not oppress others. Our children should freely express their minds to their parents without fear.

ORAP in a changed climate

"ORAP lifted us from darkness." says Elizabeth Ndlovu. But ORAP's efforts to help people achieve sustainable lives are being thwarted by both nature and macro-economics.

"The formal adoption by the Zimbabwe government of the Economic Structural Adjustment Programme in 1990/91, and the ensuing economic processes, have increased the hardships faced by communal area people," says economist Sam Moyo of the Zimbabwe Institute of Development Studies.

Drought, too, further marginalises ORAP's targeted beneficiaries, threatening to destroy their income-generating projects and wipe out their savings. "Water and food shortages will persist while the physical environment deteriorates further. There is the real risk of communal areas collapsing," says Moyo. "The abandonment of rural enterprise through migration and unsustainable survival strategies is likely, and continued short-term project investment and inadequate skills will not help."

Increasingly, as a result of the drought and structural adjustment, ORAP is having to redirect its energies from development to relief work. Its institutional coherence is being undermined, and it often has to resort to short-term planning and an ad hoc system of delivery.

"My most pressing problem right now", says chief executive Sithembiso Nyoni, "is timely delivery of resources. When the women are ready to put up a granary, there is no cement. What do we do?"

She sees no end to donor dependency. "We are committed to reducing dependence on donors. But we cannot see that happen as long as this foreign debt rests heavy on our shoulders. As long as I cannot go to the treasury and ask for funds, I cannot see ourselves becoming donor-free."

Pressure for ORAP to reform has been mounting. According to Nyoni, the board has invested in a number of ventures "to develop ORAP's income, rationalise procurement of essential inputs and...stabilise markets for their products". In terms of training, there is a shift towards economic, technical and management skills. "We are in the process of restructuring ourselves," says Nyoni. "The goal is to refine our planning process, emphasising people's participation all the way."

But ORAP and its beneficiaries need external change too. Unless radical solutions are sought at national level to reverse the increasing marginalisation of Zimbabwe's communal area inhabitants, the contrasts on the road south from Harare will become ever more stark.

A Quiet Revolution

Changing social structures in rural Bangladesh

With the help of Proshika, one of Bangladesh's largest development NGOs, landless people are improving their livelihood through credit and savings schemes, claiming their rights to common land and other natural resources, and challenging the structures responsible for their poverty. **Inam Ahmed** investigates. Photographs by **Salma Siddique**.

Dawn

The paddy fields, wet from last night's monsoon shower, glow faintly in the pre-dawn false light. The full-throated croaking of frogs fills the air. From the mosque, the Moazzin's *azan* (call for prayer) comes floating over the village.

Khairun is glad to hear the *azan*. She slips out of bed without disturbing her sleeping husband and steps outside the hut. Inside her is an unaccustomed feeling of apprehension. This morning will be the beginning of a new era in her life. For the first time in 30 years of poverty, she is going to own a cow.

Khairun reaches the tubewell in the common homeyard of the village. Rasheda, Halima and Jahanara are already there. Seeing them, Khairun regains her confidence and her apprehension vanishes. Two other friends join them. The women begin their daily morning chores—feeding the babies *pantha* (last night's leftover rice dipped in water), setting free the chickens, cooking fresh rice for their husbands.

When the sun breaks over the bamboo bush in the east the six women of the village of Bihar Uttarpara in Bogra, northern Bangladesh, set out for the Proshika office two villages away. Their friends watch sceptically as they go. These women are going to buy cows—not just one or two between them, but six! They must be out of their heads!

At the Proshika office, it takes some time to deal with the formalities—signing papers and counting out the money, 60,000 Taka (US$1,500) in all. The women have never before seen such thick bundles of banknotes. Their husbands now join them and together, accompanied by a Proshika worker, they head for the market.

It is after midday when the women, leading their six cows of motley colours, and beaming with excitement, reach their home village. The villagers look on in astonishment. For Khairun and the other women, it is the most glorious day of their lives.

Unshackling the chains

Khairun and her five friends are members of a *samity* (group). Together they have saved sufficient money to be able to obtain credit and buy the six cows. Such a purchase, providing them with an independent livelihood, has the capacity to transform their lives. In many places in rural Bangladesh, women and men are taking collective action, discovering that through this they can have a say over their lives, affect others' lives and become a decisive force in society. A quiet revolution seems to be taking place.

Proshika is encouraging and assisting this revolution through its social and economic empowerment processes, at the heart of which is a programme of employment- and income-generation among the rural poor. The word "Proshika" is a compound of the first letters of the Bangla words for training, education and development action. Established in 1976, it is now one of the largest non-government organisations (NGOs) working in Bangladesh.

It has helped poor men and women to organise themselves

into *samities*, each of 15-20 members. These are federated into Village Coordination Committees (VCCs), the first tier of the bottom-up structure of Proshika's programme of Participatory Sustainable Development (PSD). "It is in these groups that the poor engage themselves in the participatory planning of their development," says Dr Qazi Faruque Ahmed, Proshika's executive director. "They plan what they need and what they want to do to improve their lot."

Proshika has outstripped government development efforts in its work in villages in Singair Union, Manikganj District, and Shibganj Union, northern Bogra. (Bangladesh's administrative system is similar but not identical to India's. The country is divided into Districts; these are divided into *thanas*, which are subdivided into Unions. In turn, Unions are made up of a number of villages.)

The *samities* enjoy collateral-free, low-interest loans which would have been unthinkable within the parameters of the government's lending programme. While the government's education drive has not met its targets, *samity* members are attending adult education classes and their children go to *samity* schools. Where the government's effort to revamp the mainstream economy has been viewed with scepticism, the informal rural economy in these villages is thriving on Proshika's employment-generation programmes.

There are over 650,000 members in Proshika-supported *samities*, half of them women, based in over 5,000 villages. Proshika estimates that nearly 4 million people have benefited from its activities: 50 million trees have been planted, 30,000 houses for the homeless constructed, 10,000 tubewells sunk and 76,000 latrines installed; 1.5 million people have received training and 300 non-formal primary schools have been set up. By the end of 1993, Proshika had disbursed 46,431 loans totalling 895 million Taka (US$22,375,000), an average of 19,276 Taka (US$482).

The success of the PSD programme is affecting villagers outside Proshika's intervention areas. People are trying to emulate the *samities* and their activities. Local leaders and government officials are becoming more positive about the poverty alleviation schemes and the endeavours of group members.

Rural poverty and Proshika's response

The country in which Proshika works is the world's most densely populated large country. With an area of 144,000 sq km and a population of over 114 million in 1992, this gives a density of 792 people per sq km. Four out of five people live in rural areas, and more than half of them own no land. The population is growing by 2.3% a year [1]. Small farms—already too small to feed a family—are shrinking still further, and an increasing number of smallholders are losing their land.

Fewer than one in four people can read, and five out of six women are illiterate. Infant mortality is high by international standards (125 per 1,000 live births), and life expectancy only 52.2 years. Only 60% of the population have access to health services and 32% to some form of sanitation.

Bangladesh is one of the most fertile lands on the earth. Flooded every year by the Brahmaputra and the Ganges, which deposit rich silt over nearly the whole land, much of the country can support three crops of rice a year. Yet Bangladesh is the fifth poorest country in terms of per capita GNP, which has been growing at only 0.4% a year.

The main explanation for this dichotomy is the huge inequality of land and wealth distribution. The 50% of the population with less than half an acre (0.2 hectares) of land—technically landless—are left at the mercy of village elites, the *jotdars* and *matbars*, for their employment. Many of the poor are tenants, working a sharecropping system, giving up a proportion of the crop they grow to the landowner. All this discourages investment in improvements such as irrigation and leads to low productivity. The extreme poverty leads to low rural demand, which discourages the establishment of other business activities, particularly in the rural areas.

More than 16 million people (excluding farmers' families) still work in agriculture as farmers, tenants or labourers, while fewer than a million work in formal sector industry.

Proshika's work is above all directed towards supporting the poor in activities which, even in small ways, challenge and undermine the inequitable structures of society. "Poverty is caused not because poor people want to remain passive about their situation", says Dr Faruque, "but because the structure of society, based on dominance and dependence, is such that the cards are stacked against them and the traditional trickle-down development process has left them in the cold. The people are poor because they are in chains. Proshika is unshackling the chains by empowering the poor, by increasing their participation in their development process."

"The *khas* land is ours"

The task seemed formidable to the poor women of Madhya Chargram Mahila Samity in Singair Thana—to win back a large area of *khas* (state-owned) land occupied illegally by the village *matbars* (elites). "But we knew we had a full right to the *khas* land," says Kulsum Begum, assistant secretary of the *samity*. "We learnt from Proshika's human development training course that the country's law gives priority to the landless to enjoy the *khas* land."

For the landless members of the *samity*, this stretch of land, just across a narrow stream, would mean a respectable place to live. They would no longer have to beg the *jotdars* (large landowners) to spare them a 10-foot-square (about one sq metre) piece of land to build a hut for the whole family. They would never again have to sell their labour to the *jotdars* at the unbelievably low rate of 15 Taka (38 US cents) a day, just to be allowed to stay on the land. Acquiring the *khas* land would free the landless women from serfdom.

"So, the *samity* members sat together to discuss how to get control of the *khas* land," says Kulsum, years of hardship visible in her skeletal figure. After much debate, they decided to invite the *jotdars* to a meeting, and simply ask them to relinquish the land.

The *samity* members only half-believed this would work. But on the appointed day the women of Chargram village thronged the venue. Their husbands and other men from various local groups came too. There was a sizeable crowd. Somebody managed to provide a table, and some chairs for the *jotdars* to sit on. Soon the *jotdars* arrived with the current chairman and former chairman of Singair Union and the conference began.

"I delivered the first speech," recalls Kulsum. "Seeing the big

Being able to build homes on reclaimed *khas* land, and having a small plot of land to cultivate, can free landless women from serfdom.

crowd of landless poor, I was no longer nervous or doubtful about our success. We told them one by one that the *khas* land was ours. The *jotdars* had been enjoying it for a long time, but now we wanted it. We threatened...that if they did not allow us into the *khas* land, we would use force."

"After hearing them, we knew they were right about the *khas* land," says Ramizuddin, the former chairman of the Union. "We knew it would be futile trying to stop them, as this would have only led to bloodshed. They were united and determined."

The women went home triumphant. The next morning, the *jotdars'* houses on the *khas* land were dismantled and new huts went up for the landless poor. They had found a new meaning to life, and had rediscovered their self-respect so long buried under the insults of the *jotdars*.

"I am no longer haunted by dreams that the *jotdars* are forcing me out of my hut," says Jamila Khatun. "I am now free from forced labour and I am self-employed in a cow-fattening project. My husband has taken out a loan from Proshika and is running a small business. I have a vegetable garden that also supports my family." Jamila has also taken out 9,000 Taka (US$225) loan from Proshika for her new house. "It doesn't leak in the monsoon any more and we do not have to spend sleepless nights when it rains."

Other Proshika-supported groups are gaining possession of public resources such as *khas* lands and ponds, seasonally flooded land, roadsides, embankment slopes and denuded forest land.

"Access to public resources gives the poor—deprived for centuries—a solid sense of worth," says Dr Faruque. "So far, Proshika groups have been successful in exercising rightful control over 26,000 acres [10,520 hectares] of denuded forest land and 4,000 km of stripland [roadsides, embankment slopes and railway track sides] where they have planted 49.15 million trees. Besides, they are doing aquaculture and fishing in over 300 *khas* ponds and 50 km of river.... They exercise control over irrigation water—both ground and surface water—and manage irrigation services to 30,000 acres [12,140 hectares] of land and receive one fourth of the crop as a fee."

However, the landless often still find themselves in conflict with the *jotdars* who are reluctant to forego the benefits they have enjoyed for so long. Demgara Pashwimpara Bhumihin Samity, is one group which is still battling for its rights.

"We had taken out a lease on 2.2 acres [0.9 hectare] of *khas* land in 1987," says Nabiruddin, a member of the *samity*. "In 1992, we decided in our group meeting to go for fish farming and started digging a big pond on the *khas* land." But a member of the *samity* who was also the chairman of the Pond Implementation Committee embezzled 10,000 Taka (US$250) from the group fund. The project was about to collapse when the other 15 members of the group offered their voluntary labour and completed the task of digging the pond.

"Then we needed some money to pump water into the pond and to buy fish fry. So, we asked the Implementation Committee chairman to return our money. It was then that the trouble started," recalls Nabiruddin. The chairman left the *samity* and banded up with some *jotdars* in the village who had had an eye on the *khas* land for years.

Another *samity* member, Bablu Mondol, takes over the story: "It was lunchtime when we heard that the *jotdars* had set up a deep tubewell and were filling the pond with water. It took us just five minutes to organise 40 men and women, each armed with machetes and bamboo sticks, and we rushed to the pond."

"The *jotdars* were a 25-man team," continues Bakshi. "They tried to bluff us by saying that the government had cancelled the lease to the poor. We challenged them, but they would not listen." Fighting broke out. It took the landless poor 15 minutes to drive away the *jotdars* and their force.

"That night we called a *shalis* [village court]...to settle the issue," recalls Nabiruddin. "The *jotdars* reiterated their claim that the lease had been cancelled." As the *shalis* failed to settle the conflict, the *samity* has now filed a case in the state court against the *jotdars*.

Where *samities* have won control of *khas* land they often go into fish farming.

Forging unity and strength

"Alone we are helpless, but together we are powerful." This is the realisation of Nazran Banu of Singair Thana. "My *samity* has united the landless poor...and has given us the strength to challenge the evil *matbars* in the village."

Dr Faruque explains that Proshika sees an important link between the local unity of the poor and "activities that, in providing a degree of material independence, assist the poor in counteracting the structures responsible for their poverty". In this sense, Proshika's activities are mutually reinforcing. "These activities include group formation, conscientisation through informal processes of development education, and social action on issues such as just wages, and access to common resources."

Samity members contribute a certain sum of money to the group fund every week. "My *samity* has 15 members," says Shukur Jan of Mollapara Mahila Samity in Azimpur village, Singair. "We contribute 3 Taka [7.5 US cents] every week. In two months...we managed savings of 150 Taka [US$3.75]. In another six to seven months, we will take loans from Proshika."

It takes a group nine months of active existence to qualify for loans. To apply, a group must have about 20% of the loan amount as savings. Individual or collective projects can be financed. In the case of individually implemented activities such as cattle fattening, rice husking, small trading, vegetable gardening and poultry rearing, the loans are distributed by the groups to the individual members. Collectively implemented projects include fish culture, irrigation and rural industries.

"My group received a 30,000 Taka [US$750] loan for a cow-fattening project," says Aklima Khatun of Madhya Chargram. "Five of us purchased cows with the money and reared them for three months. Then we sold the cows and made a profit of 12,000 Taka [US$300]. Half this profit went to the *samity's* fund and the other half was divided between the five of us."

Suffering from a stomach ulcer and unable to work in the fields, Bazlur Rashid of Madhya Chargram in Singair despaired of finding a suitable job. Today, with a 3,000 Taka (US$75)

Weaving is one of several rural industries supported by Proshika loans.

Proshika loan, he is happily running his own sericulture (silkworm-rearing) business. "I can earn about 6,000 Taka (US$150) a year," says Rashid. "My business is still small. Next year, I will double my investment."

Democracy from the base

Group members themselves do all the planning for their future programmes. These may be for employment- and income-generating projects or for social development activities. The latter can include setting up primary schools and adult literacy centres, increasing children's enrolment in schools, or campaigning against practices such as payment of dowry or for rights over public resources.

The *samity* comes to a consensus about future projects which it then presents to the Village Coordination Committee (VCC). This body discusses all the projects, checks the funds needed to implement them and then sends the proposals on to the Union Coordination Committee (UCC), which consists of representatives of all the VCCs in a Union. After further refinement, the projects then go to the Thana Coordination

Committee (TCC) which meets once a year, coordinates all the plans from different groups and finally forwards these to the Proshika head office for funding.

The head office disburses the funds required to the regional Proshika offices which provide them as loans to the groups. "We never quarrel over who [is] to get loans first," says Abul Hussain of Panchadas village, Bogra. "We always take the decision together in the group meetings and everybody knows that anyone who doesn't get a loan this time, will get it soon."

"This is a unique situation even in the national context where the uneducated poor, always used as a vote bank by the local politicians, are practising democracy," says Dr Faruque. "Through such practices, they become conscious of their rights and, as a result, they often refuse to vote for money in the national elections. This has a good and far-reaching impact on both politics and development, because the politicians then realise that if they want to win over the people, money alone will not do. They have to work for the development of the poor."

"Proshika directs loans to the poor through the groups because this also ensures repayment of the money," says Abedin of Proshika's Singair office. "The group members always remain alert, so that no one defaults. If one member defaults, the group compensates from their savings."

"This really acts like magic," says Dr Faruque. "Look at the national figures—40% of all loans turn into bad debt. But our loan recovery rate is 96%."

The Mahila Samity of Char Nayadingi village once had to repay Proshika's loan from its own fund. "We had taken out a 75,000 Taka [US$1,875] loan from Proshika for a cow-fattening project," says Insan Bibi. "We could have made a good profit from the project, but one of our members, Jamlia, lost her money in the cattle market. So, in the end, we had to repay this money from the *samity's* fund."

The government and opposition parties have encouraged this loan default culture in the past, trying to muster votes by promising to waive loans. The present Bangladesh National Party (BNP) government, after coming to power, declared a waiver on agricultural loans of up to 5,000 Taka (US$125).

"Such steps corrupt the rural poor," says an official of the Bangladesh Rural Development Board (BRDB), the state-owned organisation that also works among the rural poor. "They take it for granted that loans will always be waived. Even my organisation is facing problems with retrieving loans from the poor, who say that since BRDB is a government organisation operating among the poor, their loans should also be waived in keeping with the government's decision."

For Proshika *samities*, money does not come free. Every Taka they take from Proshika, they have to pay back with interest. "We pay 14% interest on loans for buying vegetable seeds", says Khorshed Alam of Madhya Chargram, "and 5% for housing loans. We really don't mind the interest rate because we used to have to take loans at much higher rates than this from the *mahajans* [moneylenders]." These can be as high as 120%.

Anwara Begum took a 5,000 Taka (US$125) loan for a cow-fattening project at 10% interest. "I paid another 5% as an insurance premium so that if the cow dies, I will not lose the money. Proshika will bear the loss."

From paddy trader to vet

With Proshika's assistance, some individuals have launched themselves on entirely new careers. Ekram Hussain, aged 32, widely known as Vet Ekram, has done just this and is now the most popular person in the remote village of Buriganj, Shibganj Union. Ekram is a paraveterinary doctor who learnt his trade from Proshika's human development training centre.

"I was a nobody three years back," Ekram says. "No one knew me. No one ever bothered to offer me a *salaam* [Muslim greeting]. But today if my shop is closed for a day, people start enquiring if I am sick." Ekram tells his story while sitting inside his shop, which is situated opposite a cattle bazaar. Behind him, the wooden racks display a range of livestock medicines. On the table in front of him are packets of a special cow diet.

"I am a member of Panchadas Bakra Bhumihin Samity of Proshika," continues Vet Ekram. "I was a small paddy trader. The income was barely enough to support my family. A young man from my village first attended Proshika's *samaj unnyan* [social development] training and he inspired us to form the society."

A few days later, Ekram attended a training course on vaccination at the Shibganj Proshika office and started working as a vaccinator. A few months later, he had the opportunity to do more advanced veterinary training, at Proshika's centre at Koitta, Manikganj. "I came back as a paravet and opened my first clinic in Jamurhat village," recalls Ekram. "In three years, I became well-known...and it even reached Buriganj village across the river. I was in great demand there and the people started urging me to set up shop in Buriganj." Finally, Ekram rented a shop for 120 Taka (US$3) a month in Buriganj and started his practice.

"I started going around the village, vaccinating poultry and cattle. Before I came, people had to go to Sadar Union, far away from here, to get vaccines or medicines from the government vet

A paravet who trained at a Proshika centre innoculates a cow.

office. They were very glad to have me here. The demand was so high that I stopped going around the village. Instead, people came to my shop to get medicines for their animals and birds."

There is a fully qualified vet in Buriganj, but the villagers prefer Ekram. They say he behaves like one of them, can be reached at any time and hurries to a client's home whenever he is needed. "He is equally expert and charges lower fees", says one villager. "He even takes vegetables or chickens in return for his services."

His expertise has brought Ekram financial rewards: "I have built a two-storey house replacing the shanty. I am sending my elder son to school. I have my own tubewell and furniture. Unless I had had the training from Proshika, I would still be the poor Ekram that I was."

Impact on the labour market

More widespread and successful self-employment also has an important effect on the employment market.

A year ago, the landless of Char Nayadingi village, in Singair Union, were lucky if they could get 10 Taka (25 US cents) and a meal for a day's work in the crop fields. Today they feel no temptation to take jobs paying 50 Taka (US$1.25) plus a meal.

"There were few jobs in the village and too many landless grappling to get work," says Abu Kaiser. "The *mahajans* and *jotdars* used to take advantage of this situation and offered us anything for working from dawn to dusk. We had no choice. If we asked for more, they would say: 'If it does not suit, then you can go. There is no shortage of workers.'"

The downtrodden people vied with each other to be hired for the entire harvesting season, because a harvesting contract meant two months' assured work. "Sometimes we were forced to work for the *jotdars* because we owed them money," says Ismail of Bogra. "Any loan...was tied to forced work during the harvesting season, and in such cases, our wages were even lower."

Harun-ur-Rashid of Damgara village, Shibpur Union, recalls: "The *jotdars* used to contract us months before the harvesting season began and fixed our wages in rice, not in money, when the commodity was at its peak price. But after the harvest, the rice price would drop, but we were still paid the same quantity of rice.

So we were deprived of our just wages."

But things started changing after the landless united in *samities*. With loans from Proshika, members found new activities of their own, such as trading, cow fattening or vegetable gardening. "When we had enough work in our hands, we no longer needed to work for others. We have our own jobs," Rashed Mia says. "So, the *jotdars* and *mahajans* started finding it hard to get labourers at 10 Taka a day."

The wage now varies between 50 and 70 Taka a day (US$1.25-1.75) depending on the demand for labour, but few people are interested even in these higher rates.

"The *mahajans* now come and request us to work in their fields," says Bablu Mondol of Bogra. "Sometimes, we work for them just out of mercy, sometimes out of good neighbourly feelings. But I tell you, their days of exploitation are over."

Even local governments in these areas face a shortage of funds for their development work because of higher wage levels. "Labour costs have gone up here," says Dewan Mazharul Huq, chairman of Singair Union. "The government's allocation for wages is five kilos of wheat a day, which is equivalent to 25 Taka [62.5 US cents]. But the minimum wage a worker now demands is...as high as 50 Taka [US$1.25] plus a meal. Now I will be facing problems if the government does not increase its fund allocation. Many of my development projects like road construction are lying half-done...."

The poor: "a recognisable force"

In conservative Muslim Bangladeshi society, which is controlled by patriarchal norms, Kulsum Begum is surely an exception. A diminutive lady in her 40s, Kulsum is probably the only woman who is an executive committee member of a *madrasa* (Muslim school). "My *samity* is very powerful in the village," says Kulsum who is also the assistant secretary of Madhya Chargram Mahila Samity in Singair. "Since the *samity* started seven years ago, all the members have found employment in income-generating projects. We have even acquired *khas* lands from the village *matbars* for the landless."

It was apparent to the committee members of Nur-Ya-Ashraful

In conservative Muslim society women are among the most disadvantaged. But women's *samities* are beginning to change power relationships.

Madrasa that without the cooperation of the landless poor, it would be hard to run the *madrasa*. "It was the *samity* which first proposed to the committee that the *madrasa* should have a female representative, and they selected me," says Kulsum. The committee was shocked. But one member, Hamid, came to see the logic. "He convinced the *madrasa* people that I should be taken on to the committee because then it would be easy to persuade the *samity* members to send their children to the *madrasa* for education," smiles Kulsum.

Mohammed Rajab Ali of Azimpur village in Singair is another rarity. Once a small shopkeeper among many others, Ali is today a member of Singair Union Parishad (UP), the local administration. More interestingly, Ali did not have to spend a Taka of his own to win the post: it is an unwritten rule in the country that votes have to be bought.

Ali is also the president of Proshika's TCC and as a representative of the landless he always tries to uphold their rights in UP meetings. "It is the landless poor who persuaded me to contest the UP election," Ali says with a shy smile. "I was too shaky to stand for election. I told my villagers how can I, a small fish , ever stand against the big fish? But they would not listen, they were in a crazy mood. So they canvassed for me and voted me to the post."

Ali now sits side by side with people of much higher social standing than himself. "All the other members are rich people," he says." If I were not a member, they would have thrown me out of the room for sitting with them." Having been elected to the post, Ali has not forgotten his poor supporters and tries to help them in every way that he can.

"We had a meeting the other day to fix the licence fee for the rickshaws. The chairman and other members said the fee should be 100 Taka [US$2.50] a year. But I said it is too high for the poor rickshaw-pullers and proposed...30 Taka [75 US cents]. Later the fee was lowered to 35 Taka [88 US cents]." Similarly, Ali fought successfully to keep tax on small shopkeepers down to 100 Taka (US$2.50) a year after a proposed rise to 500 Taka (US$12.50).

Ali also represents the poor in any *shalis* and ensures justice for them. "The poor people come and request me to be present in the *shalis* so that the rich cannot arrange a mock trial. Because of my position, the rich cannot brush aside my observations."

Like Kulsum and Rajab Ali, the poor are gaining more and more control in society because they are being organised into groups. "The poor are emerging as a recognisable force in society," says Dr Faruque. "They can no longer be ignored and once they can gain a social space for themselves, they can act independently for their own betterment. In this way they unshackle the chains of poverty."

Changing power relationships

The members of Krishak Samity from Char Nayadingi village are involved in vegetable farming. "When the time came for sowing seeds, we took a loan from Proshika at 14%...now we are free of these bloodsuckers [the *mahajans*]," says Abu Taleb.

"One major reason for poor farmers becoming marginal is the high interest rates and the *bandhaki* [mortgage] system of land," explains Dr Faruque. "The *mahajans* take over the land if the farmers fail to repay the loans on time. Given the high rate of interest [as much as 120%], loan repayment is usually a tough job." Not only have the poor been able to avoid their dependence on the *mahajans*, but the elites now often come to the poor for loans!

"The *matbars* of our village often come to us and take loans from the *samity's* fund," says Islam of Char Nayadingi Krishak Samity. "We give them loans at 80% interest. Last month, Kanchi Matbar needed money to send his son abroad. So he took a loan from us." This practice often takes place in secret, although it is strictly forbidden under Proshika rules to lend to anyone other than *samity* members.

Rajab Ali of Azimpur Shramik Samity in Singair is a shopkeeper. He says, "Before, the wholesalers would not give me commodities on credit because they felt that I had no credibility. They could not depend on me in case I went broke. Now I am a *samity* member. I have a cash fund and I can purchase in cash. But the big difference is that I can now buy more on credit because the *mahajans* no longer feel that I am a small isolated businessman."

"A kind of ownership"

The engine thuds rhythmically, and water gushes out of the Chinese Deep Tubewell (DTW) pump to reach the green paddy fields of Barotopa village in Gazipur District. This irrigation pump has brought a new kind of strength to the landless of the village. It has allowed them control over a natural resource—water—and given them access to, and use of, other people's land. They have become the watersellers of Barotopa village.

Two groups, the Bhai Bhai Bhumihin Samity and Bhumihin Daridra Samity, operate the irrigation system together. "We took out a 92,000 Taka [US$2,300] loan from Proshika and purchased the tubewell for 52,000 Taka [US$1,300]," says Rahim Ali of the Bhai Bhai Samity. "The remaining 40,000 Taka [US$1,000] was so that we could cover the operating costs for the first season."

The *samity* members had no land of their own to irrigate. So, they came to an agreement with the *jotdars* to irrigate their land in return for 25% of the crop harvested. Rafique and his fellow group members now operate two DTWs, watering 20 hectares of crop land.

"When we first sank the wells, most landowners did not want our service," says Rafique. "But we convinced some farmers, dug water channels and supplied them with water." The benefits of irrigation were obvious because high-yield varieties of rice need good irrigation for a good harvest. Soon more farmers began to subscribe to the watersellers. "In two years, we paid off the loans," says Rafique. "This year each *samity* member had 10 maunds [380 kg] of rice as crop share and the *samity* received 39,000 Taka [US$975] by selling the rice."

Like the landless of Barotopa and Singair, hundreds of Proshika group members are today operating 350 DTWs all over the country, irrigating over 12,000 hectares of crop land. "This is a unique way of establishing the poor's right over other people's lands," says Dr Faruque. "They had no land on which to grow crops. But by gaining control over water, they also gained a kind of ownership over land and crops. It took us 10 years of research to evolve this system."

Mosammat Nurjahan working in the tree nursery started by her *samity*. Social forestry and ecological agriculture are becoming increasingly popular.

"These are our trees"

Prakirtik krishi (ecological agriculture) and *samajik banajan* (social forestry) are becoming more and more popular among *samity* members. The landless of the country, often accused of destroying the environment by cutting down trees indiscriminately or overusing the land, have proved the injustice of the accusation. Given not only the necessary training but also rights over trees and land, the poor today zealously protect the environment. Although they may never have heard of the greenhouse effect or soil contamination, they are helping to preserve the planet.

If you walk through rural areas of Singair, you are bound to notice the young trees growing on both sides of the roads. Proshika groups have taken leases on roadside *khas* land, bought and planted saplings, and now look after the trees with motherly care.

Rahela Khatun, a middle-aged woman, sits in the shade of a 10-foot-high (2-metre) tree, weaving a mat. In front of her, a yellow flag flutters in the wind. "These are our trees," Rahela points proudly at the roadside trees. "My *samity* planted 1,500 trees two years ago on a one-and-a-half kilometre stretch along the road." Rahela is a caretaker of these trees, her job symbolised by the yellow flag. She and two other women of the Mollapara Mahila Samity of Azimpur village in Singair guard the trees so that no one can destroy them. In return, they receive five kilos of wheat a day from Proshika.

The groups lease the *khas* lands on condition that when the trees are sold for turning into furniture some 20 years later, the local government authorities will get half the money. The groups either buy the saplings from Proshika or grow them in *samity* nurseries. "Only the wheat is given free to the caretakers," says Abedin of the Singair Proshika office. "Proshika gets the wheat from the World Food Programme for distribution among the poor and we distribute this wheat to the caretakers of the trees."

The caretakers will get their daily ration of wheat for the first three years after planting. After that the trees will be too big to be destroyed by cattle or people. The whole village will then take care of them. "Another 20 years, and we will be the richest women in the village," says Rahela. "These are costly...trees and when they grow, my group might earn as much as 2 crore Taka [US$500,000] by selling them. We trim the branches of the trees regularly and they serve as firewood for us. If 2 crore Taka is too far away, the branches are our immediate return."

The social forestry programme of the groups has stimulated another kind of activity in the villages. As demand for tree saplings has increased, the group members have set up their own nurseries.

Three and a half years ago, Mosammat Nurjahan of Barabazar village in Bogra was a housewife. "Looking after the children, keeping the house tidy, cooking and trying to keep my husband happy, these [tasks] were my day's work," says Nurjahan. Then she became a member of Barabazar Milon Mahila Samity and, together with other members, started a nursery.

"But we had no land or money", says Nurjahan, taking a break from her work in the nursery, "so we took a 15,000 Taka [US$375] loan from Proshika and leased some land for 6,000 Taka [US$150]." It was hard work for the *samity* women to prepare seed beds, sell plants in the market and take meticulous care of the plants. "We did it all by ourselves and we took wages for the work from the loan amount," Nurjahan says.

Husbands also joined in the work, and took responsibility for selling plants in the market. Plants are sold both to groups in the village and to individual customers. "It took us two years to repay the loan, and then we again borrowed 54,000 Taka [US$1,350] for expansion of the nursery," says Nurjahan.

Rokeya has been busy filling polythene bags with cow dung mixed with earth. "We get 5 Taka [12 US cents] for filling every 100 bags," she says. "We can fill as many as 1,000 bags a day. In the beginning, my husband was very annoyed at my working in the nursery. But we needed money and once I started earning it, he became quiet."

Ecological farming is also becoming popular. "We now make our own natural fertiliser by decomposing [and mixing] cow dung, hay and water hyacinths," says Nazran Banu of Madhya Chargram village, Singair. "We don't use chemical fertiliser any more." For pesticide, they make a kind of potion with leaves of the neem tree, tobacco and cow urine. "We learnt these tricks on Proshika's training courses," says Lutfur Rahman of Madhya Chargram. "This is as good as any pesticide. It helps us in two ways—we don't have to spend money on chemicals and it doesn't harm our environment."

Sustaining the process

The crucial question facing Proshika is whether the activities of the *samities* are sustainable. In particular, are group members sufficiently motivated to continue their efforts independently of Proshika's intervention? Sirajul Islam, Proshika's principal programme coordinator, explains that this is Proshika's aim. "Once groups become self-sustaining and independent", he says, "the task of poverty reduction will become easier."

Ten years ago, 22 landless poor set up the Purba Jahangirabad Bhumihin Samity in Bogra with no savings at all. Today, the *samity* has 175,000 Taka (US$4,375) in cash, and assets of 180 rickshaw vans, 1,500 high-value trees in a social forestry project, a half-hectare banana plantation and a large house for the *samity*. The group has paid off all its loans and aims to undertake more employment-generating projects.

"Our first project of potato seed preservation started with a loan of 70,000 Taka [US$1,750] from Proshika," explains Ismail Hossain, secretary of the *samity*. "Within a year, we paid off the loan and took fresh loans for buying rickshaw vans and starting rice-husking projects. Our last loan was for small business development. Today, we do not owe a single Taka to Proshika or anyone. We will not be taking any fresh loans because the existing projects can support the group members very well." Each member can now earn 2,000 Taka (US$50) a month from the projects.

Maddha Jahangirabad Bhumihin Samity has savings of 50,000 Taka (US$1,250). "We do not need loans any more," says *samity* member Mohammed Abdul Hossain. "Even if Proshika now withdraws from the village, we will be taking on new projects from...our own funds."

Saleha is a member of Madhya Chargram Mahila Samity in Singair. "I took a 5,000 Taka [US$125] loan for a cow-fattening project and sold the cow for 8,000 Taka [US$200]. The profit I gave to my husband for business. He is now engaged in a bamboo business and since his income is good, I haven't taken out any further loans."

Anwara Begum of Singair says: "We have learnt from Proshika how to form groups, how to keep groups together and how to invest in projects for employment. Even if Proshika were no longer here, we would carry on the task for our own sake. Because without the group, there is no strength for us."

In Shibganj Union alone there are 50 groups with savings of over 20,000 Taka (US$500) and seven groups with savings of 60,000 Taka (US$1,500). Proshika defines a self-sufficient group as one that has savings of at least 60,000 Taka, needs no outside credit and where members are earning at least 1,000 Taka (US$25) a month. Proshika is carrying out a study on self-sufficiency and estimates that at least 300 groups are now self-sufficient.

A national task

The rapid transformation of the situation of *samity* members from stark poverty to solvency has had an effect on people both within and outside Proshika's intervention areas. Seeing the development process at work has brought a shift in people's views about group formation and NGO activities from an extremely negative to a positive position.

"Although I am a poor marginal farmer, I did not wish to join the Proshika *samity* in my village," says Abul Kalam Azad, a wiry man in his 30s from Bihar Uttar Para village in Shibganj. "I could not believe that the poor could ever do anything." But as the years went by, Kalam's opinions changed. "I felt like a fool as I found that the *samity* members were all working on income-generating projects with Proshika loans. Then I also wanted to be a member of the *samity*. But the members said they did not want to increase their membership."

Kalam was undeterred. "I myself started a *samity* a year back with my brothers," he says. "I just copied the activities of Proshika and started with three Taka a week savings per member." Slowly, other villagers joined him and the membership of Kalam's group increased to 15. "We already have a 2,000 Taka

[US$50] fund from our weekly savings. When the fund gets a little bigger, we will start projects like cow-fattening or buy a rickshaw van."

Khodeja Begum of Gobinder village, Singair, was prevented by her husband, Halimhad, from joining the *samity*. "He said NGOs corrupt ladies and...suck out money from the poor," explains Khodeja. After a few years, Halimhad changed his mind and himself insisted that Khodeja join the women's group. "But to join the group, I had to deposit the equivalent savings of every existing group member," says Khodeja, "and I do not have that much money." She is now waiting for a new group to be formed in her village.

Ramizuddin Ahmed, former chairman of Singair Union and a local *jotdar*, says: "When Proshika first started their group formation here, we were sceptical about their activities. We thought that the NGO and the poor would together create anarchy in the village. But soon we found out that the groups were doing good things. Unemployed men and women who used to loiter around, some of them engaged in petty theft, became productive and socially conscious. So we now try to help them whenever we can."

The secretary of the Singair Union branch of the Communist Party of Bangladesh, advocate Mohammed Abdul Huq Khan, finds Proshika's approach quite different from his own party's line of thinking. "Proshika does not influence the people politically. Rather it is helping the left-outs of society," he says. "But I think it should discuss its development programmes more openly with local leaders and politicians and should seek their participation in development."

"My notion about NGOs was that they make people dependent on loans and that most of their money is wasted on Pajeros [four-wheel drive vehicles]," says an official in the Thana administration. "But my experience in Singair, Dhamrai and other places is different from what I used to think. Proshika is turning the hands of the poor into productive tools. Now I believe, without NGO intervention it is impossible to eradicate poverty in our country."

"We are politically antagonistic to NGOs because we see them as the new East India Company," declares Mohammed Abdul Kader, general secretary of Singair Thana Jatiya Party (the third largest opposition party in the country). "But what I find here is that Proshika is giving new life to the poor. Nobody in society had ever bothered to look at them, but now, these poor are overcoming their poverty. This is a national task done by Proshika."

Dusk

Fifteen men are gathered in the open space in the centre of Azimpur village after dinner. The light from the kerosene lamp dances on their shiny work-tired faces. Tonight is the Azimpur Shramik Samity's meeting to discuss what new projects the members should start next year. One says they should buy a power tiller, but many disagree because this involves too much money. After some discussion it is agreed that they will go for small businesses and vegetable gardening.

After about an hour, the men return to their huts to sleep. They have come a long way from poverty and nothingness. But for the villagers of Azimpur, there is no looking back any more.

Appendix 1

A proposed action agenda for the Social Summit

● Approve a world social charter as a new social contract among all nations and all people.

● Endorse a new development paradigm of sustainable human development—with economic growth centred on people and sustainable from one generation to the next.

● Give the United Nations the mandate to draw up a comprehensive blueprint for ensuring global human security and protecting people from threats in their daily lives— poverty, unemployment, drugs, terrorism, environmental degradation and social disintegration.

● Agree on a targeted reduction of 3% a year in global military spending for the decade 1995-2005, and direct that a certain proportion of these potential savings—say, 20% by industrial countries and 10% by developing countries—be credited to a global human security fund.

● Approve a human development compact for the next 10 years (1995-2005) whereby all nations pledge to ensure the basic human development levels for all their people, and endorse the 20:20 proposal requiring developing nations and aid donors to earmark a minimum of 20% of their budgets for human priority concerns.

● Recommend to ECOSOC [The United Nations Economic and Social Council] that it examine the feasibility of various forms of global taxation—especially taxes on global pollution and on speculative movements of capital—to raise adequate financing for setting up a new global fund for human security.

● Urge the international community to strengthen the role of the United Nations in the socio-economic field and to vest more decision-making powers in the UN by establishing an Economic Security Council to manage the new dimensions of global human security.

Source: UNDP, *Human Development Report 1994*, Oxford University Press, New York, 1994.

Appendix 2

A new world social charter

- We the people of the world solemnly pledge to build a new global civil society, based on the principles of equal opportunity, rule of law, global democratic governance and a new partnership among all nations and all people.

- We propose to build a society where the right to food is as sacrosanct as the right to vote, where the right to a basic education is as deeply enshrined as the right to a free press and where the right to development is considered one of the fundamental human rights.

- We collectively pledge to build new foundations of human security, which ensure the security of people through development, not arms; through cooperation, not confrontation; through peace not war. We believe that no provision in the Charter of the United Nations will ever ensure global security unless people have security in their homes, in their jobs, in their communities and in their environment.

- We are fully convinced that diversity in our societies is our strength, not our weakness, and we intend to protect this diversity by ensuring non-discrimination between all our people, irrespective of gender, race, religion or ethnic origin.

- We collectively believe that our world cannot survive one-fourth rich and three-fourths poor, half democratic and half authoritarian, with oases of human development surrounded by deserts of human deprivation. We pledge to take all necessary actions, nationally and globally, to reverse the present trend of widening disparities within and between nations.

- We are convinced that it is possible to overcome the worst aspects of poverty in our lifetime through collective effort. We jointly affirm that our first step towards this goal will be to design a global compact that ensures that no child goes without an education, no human being is denied primary health care or safe drinking water and all willing couples are able to determine the size of their own families.

- We are conscious of our responsibility to present generations and to future generations, and we are determined to pass on to our children a rich natural heritage and an environment sustained and whole.

- We intend to design a pattern of development cooperation based on open global markets, not protectionism; on an equitable sharing of market opportunities, not charity; on an open policy dialogue between sovereign nations, not coercion.

- We pledge our deep commitment to a new social and economic philosophy that puts people at the centre of our concerns and creates unbreakable bonds of human solidarity.

- We strongly believe that the United Nations must become the principle custodian of our global human security. Towards this end, we are determined to strengthen the development role of the United Nations and to give it wide-ranging decision-making powers in the socio-economic field by establishing an Economic Security Council.

Source: UNDP, *Human Development Report 1994*, Oxford University Press, New York, 1994.

Appendix 3

Looking behind the clichés—common messages from the case studies

- **Communities** are not homogeneous and harmonious units. They encompass a whole range of inequalities and inequities. Even within one community group—such as women, or the poorest—there is rarely a complete consensus.

- Without gender-specific programmes it is much more difficult to achieve the equal involvement of women in participative structures.

- In trying to reach the poorest people in the community, targeting the bottom 10% but missing the bottom 5% is far better than missing the bottom 10% altogether.

- It is essential that communities are involved in evaluating their own projects. Changes that seem negligible to the outsider may constitute a real benefit for those they affect, even if they simply raise self-confidence or enable women to work a little less hard than before.

- There are always ideas from outside any situation that can stimulate community action. But real partnership will only occur when both parties feel free to accept or reject the advice and the involvement of the other. By developing clear rules of engagement both sides will know what is and is not acceptable within the flexible boundaries.

● **Participation** is about power: the power to make decisions affecting one's own life, and the life and development of the community; the power to say "no" as well as "yes". It is perhaps inevitable that the poorest are those with the least power and the greatest constraints on their ability to organise.

● Working through existing power structures allows the old elites to predominate, but to ignore the established power bases can cause great hostility which undermines or destroys the development process.

● Service provision does not itself have to be participative to be successful. Service provision is effective only if there are participative structures which enable people to define their needs and priorities.

● **Participation** takes time and energy. Until a people have enough to eat and a certain level of health they are unlikely to be able to participate effectively in the development process.

● So that participative planning can be met with the right resources at the right time, development support should be flexible, long-term and interactive. It is more important that local NGOs are able to plan confidently for the long term than that they struggle now to reach financial sustainability.

● **Income-generating programmes** can increase rather than reduce women's workload unless labour-saving devices or new approaches to the organisation of work can be introduced. Credit institutions need to take a broader look at the financing of labour-saving devices for women.

● While credit has a central role to play in the establishment and strengthening of income-generating activities, it is not enough on its own. The poorest in particular often lack confidence and experience in running small businesses, and need training, continued support and the successful example of others.

References

Preface

1. World Bank, *World Development Report 1991: The Challenge of Development*, Washington, 1991, p49.

Candles in the Wind

1. UNDP, *Human Development Report 1994*, Oxford University Press, New York, 1994.
2. Ibid.
3. Ibid.
4. Ibid.
5. Ibid.
6. Ibid.
7. Vivian, J and Maseko, G, *NGOs, Participation and Rural Development*, UNRISD Discussion Paper 49, Geneva, 1994.
8. Bunch, R, "People-centred agricultural improvement", in Haverkort, B, van der Kamp, J and Waters-Bayer, A (eds), *Joining Farmers' Experiments: Experiences in Participatory Technology Development*, IT Publications, London, 1991.
9. See, for example: Vivian, J and Maseko, G, op. cit., and Oakley, P et al., *Projects with People: The Practice of Participation in Rural Development*, International Labour Office, Geneva, 1991.
10. See, for example: Vivian, J and Maseko, G, op. cit.; Robinson, M, "Assessing the impact of NGO rural poverty alleviation programmes: evidence from South India", *Journal of International Development*, Volume 4, Number 4, 1992; and Robinson, M, "NGOs and rural poverty alleviation: implications for scaling up", in Edwards, M and Hulme, D

(eds), *Making a Difference: NGOs and Development in a Changing World*, Earthscan, London, 1992.
11. Robinson, M, op. cit.
12. Vivian, J and Maseko, G, op. cit.

From the Roots to the Sky

1. Recinos, A (translator and editor), *Popol Vuh, Historias Antiguas del Quiche*, Piedra Santa, Guatemala City, 1993.
2. CDRO, *Fundamentos de la Cosmovisión Maya*, unpublished, Guatemala City, undated, pp1-2.
3. Ministerio de Salud Pública, "Proyecto Salud y Desarrollo de la mujer indígena en Totonicapan, Solola y Quetzaltenango", *Plan de Necesidades Prioritarias de Salud en Centro-América*, Guatemala City, 1990.
4. UNDP, *Human Development Report 1994*, Oxford University Press, New York, 1994.
5. UNICEF, *Análisis de Situación del Niño y la Mujer*, SEGEPLAN, Guatemala City, 1991.
6. *Informe del Primer Semestre de 1994 de la Oficina de Derechos Humanos del Arzobispado de Guatemala*, Guatemala City, 1994, pp12-13.
7. *U K'ux Wuj*, CDRO, Guatemala City, 1994, pp1-2.
8. Asamblea de la Sociedad Civil, *Identidad y Derechos de los Pueblos Indígenas*, conference report, Guatemala City, July 1994.
9. Recinos, A, op. cit.
10. Consejo Nacional de Planificación Económica, *Análisis Interpretativo de la Situación Actual del Departamento de Totonicapan*, SEGEPLAN, Guatemala City, undated.
11. Recinos, A, op. cit.
12. Ibid.
13. Ibid.
14. *Situación de la Mujer Indígena en Guatemala*, report of the International Conference of Indigenous Peoples, Quetzaltenango, December 1993.
15. Recinos, A, op. cit.
16. Turgeon F, *Diagnóstico de los Grupos de Mujeres Asociadas al Programa Promoción Mujer*, CECI, Guatemala City, May 1994.
17. Recinos, A, op. cit.
18. Turgeon F, op. cit.
19. Ibid.
20. Recinos, A, op. cit.
21. Ibid.
22. CDRO, *Información sobre el Programa Artesanal*, Totonicapan, Guatemala, undated.
23. CDRO, *Programa de Salud y Medicina Natural*, Totonicapan, Guatemala, 1993.

24. SEGEPLAN/PNUD, *Prioridades Geográficas para la focalisación del Esfuerzo Gubernamental y no Gubernamental en Materia de Reducción de Pobreza*, roneo, Guatemala City, undated.
25. Recinos, A, op. cit.
26. Ibid.

Taking on the Powerful

1. *The Economic Times*, Calcutta, 13 May 1994.
2. *Ajkaal*, Calcutta, 7 August 1991.
3. Beck, T, *The Experience of Poverty: Fighting for Respect and Resources in Village India*, IT Publications, London 1994.
4. Srivastava, A, "IRDP fails to make a dent in Bengal", *Business and Political Observer*, Delhi, 27 November 1990.
5. *The Statesman*, Calcutta, 1 June 1991.
6. Beck, T, op. cit.
7. Ibid.
8. Ibid.
9. *The Statesman*, Calcutta, 1 June 1991.
10. Ibid.
11. *Economic Times*, Calcutta, December 1992.
12. Singh, K, *Times of India*, Delhi, 11 December 1993.

In Defence of Women

1. World Bank, *World Development Report 1991: The Challenge of Development*, Oxford University Press, New York, 1991.
2. Ibid.
3. UNDP, *Human Development Report 1994*, Oxford University Press, New York, 1994.
4. Ibid.
5. Mathot, N, *NGOs as Actors of Change*, Novib, The Hague, 1994.
6. ACFODE, *Survey on Women's Problems and Needs*, unpublished, Kampala, 1989.
7. World Bank, *Growing out of Poverty*, Washington, 1993.
8. Ibid.

Weathering the Crisis

1. Mathot N, *NGOs as Actors of Change*, Novib, The Hague, 1994.
2. A direct transcription of an interview on ZBC television on 1 August 1994.

A Quiet Revolution

1. World Bank, *World Development Report 1994: Infrastructure for Development*, Oxford University Press, New York, 1994.

Glossary

From the Roots to the Sky

atol	protein-rich cereal
Community Council	second level of organisation in CDRO
General Assembly	highest level of organisation in CDRO
Grassroots Group	first level of organisation in CDRO
Joju nam	promotion of women
machista	male-dominated
machismo	the culture of male supremacy
quetzal	main unit of currency (28 quetzals = US$1)
Quiche	Mayan language and culture
Subsystem	sectoral programme of CDRO

Taking on the Powerful

adivasis	members of a scheduled tribe, often referred to as "tribals"
Babu	government officer
baralak	powerful elite
barnahindu	high caste person
BDO	Block Development Officer
Block	administrative area encompassing a number of villages
CPM	Communist Party Marxist-Leninist
crore	10 million
dai	traditional midwife

datan	traditional toothbrush
gamcha	cotton towel
gherao	the practice of surrounding people until they concede to a demand
Green Revolution	greatly increased crop production dependent on use of improved seeds and high inputs of fertilisers, pesticides, etc.
haat	weekly bazaar
IRDP	Integrated Rural Development Programme
jalsa	a traditional religious dance
jatra	a traditional religious dance
khet majoor	agricultural labourer
khud	discarded rice grains
kirtan	a traditional religious dance
malik	property owner or employer
moral	*panchayat* head
paise	unit of currency (100 paise = 1 rupee)
panchayat	village government
pradhan	village leader
rupee	main unit of currency (33 rupees = US$1)
salishi	village court
samity	group
scheduled castes	lowest castes, especially "untouchables", which receive preferential treatment through certain social programmes
thana	administrative area (divided into Blocks)

In Defence of Women

NRM	National Resistance Movement, the only recognised political organisation in Uganda
RC	Resistance Council (village authority)
Sharia	Muslim law
Ugandan shilling	main unit of currency (930 shillings = US$1)
ULS	Uganda Law Society
UWFTC	Ugandan Women's Finance and Credit Trust, the credit arm of FIDA

Weathering the Crisis

GMB	Grain Marketing Board
utshwala	traditional beer
Zama	try it
Zimbabwean dollar	main unit of currency (8 dollars = US$1)

A Quiet Revolution

azan	Muslim call to prayer
ashram	centre for learning, usually under a guru
BNP	Bangladesh National Party
BRDB	Bangladesh Rural Development Board
jotdar	large landowner
khas	state-owned land
madrasa	Muslim school
mahajan	moneylender
matbar	village elite (often also a *jotdar*)
maund	a measure weighing 37 kilogrammes
Pajeros	four-wheel-drive vehicles
pantha	left-over rice
Parishad	administration
prakitirk krishi	ecological agriculture
salaam	Muslim greeting
samajik banayan	social forestry
samity	group
scheduled castes	lowest castes, especially "untouchables", which receive preferential treatment through certain social programmes
shalis	village court
Taka	main unit of currency (40 Taka = US$1)
thana	administrative area (divided into Unions)
TCC	Thana Coordinating Committee—the highest level in Proshika's structure
Union	administrative area encompassing a number of villages
UCC	Union Coordinating Committee—the second tier in Proshika's structure
VCC	Village Coordinating Committee—the first tier in Proshika's structure